Felt Jewelry

25 Pieces to Make Using a Variety of Simple Felting Techniques

TERESA SEARLE

St. Martin's Griffin
New York

FELT JEWELRY. Copyright © 2008 by Breslich & Foss Ltd. All rights reserved. Printed in China. For information, address St. Martin's Press, 175 Fifth Avenue, New York, N.Y. 10010.

www.stmartins.com

The written instructions, photographs, designs, patterns, and projects in this volume are intended for personal use of the reader and may be reproduced for that purpose only.

Library of Congress Cataloging-in-Publication Data Available Upon Request

ISBN-13: 978-0-312-38356-5
ISBN-10: 0-312-38356-8

First Edition: December 2008

10 9 8 7 6 5 4 3 2 1

contents

introduction	6	button flower brooch	36	layered circle belt	80
materials and equipment	8	african bangles	40	leaf shadow scarf	84
techniques	13	anemone ring	44	knitted neck warmer	90
decorating felt	17	chunky necklace	50	bird brooch	94
		secret love locket	54	rosy nuno scarf	98
the projects	19	abstract bangle	60	needle-punched flower	102
beaded felt bracelet	20	tower ring	64	cloud scarf	106
variation: beaded felt		flower bouquet neckpiece	66	sea-life head band	110
necklace, berry necklace		variation: flower barrette		phone or ipod case	116
and brooch	25	and brooch	71	flower brooch	120
pebble necklace	26	dahlia headdress	72		
folk art necklace	30	variation: dahlia corsage	75	templates	124
variation: folk art earrings		fluted corsage	76	index	128
and ring	33	variation: fluted flower		acknowledgments	128
tie-dye necklace	34	hair decorations	79		

introduction

For as long as I can remember felt has played some part in my creative life. As a child I loved the simplicity of its flat color, and the fact that it didn't fray when cut was a great bonus to me as a budding designer-maker.

As an adult, this feeling has continued and for a great part of my professional life I have made felt of varying kinds (and there are many ways to felt, as this book explores), combining this fabric with a love of other textile techniques. Stitching and knitting have always played a big part and felting, as a process on its own, is not always quite enough for me. I feel a great need to embellish and stitch and bead and button, using the glorious matte colors of wool felt as a foil for other creative textile processes.

The book covers many techniques and approaches for making felt and I hope that you will use these as a springboard for your own ideas and designs: suggestions are made throughout for other ideas the processes can be used to create. The ease, lightness, and adaptability of felt can be employed to make a large range of items. Its aesthetic and tactile appeal can easily be altered to suit your personal style and color sense. As long as you know the basic principles you can adapt and experiment with the processes, finding out new things for yourself. There seem to be as many ways to felt as there are felt makers, all adapting and exploring new ways of making this amazing and versatile fabric, so you could well discover and invent new ways of making felt, too.

TERESA SEARLE

materials and equipment

Felt and wool fibers

There are three main sources of felt, and the type you use will depend on the project you are making and your personal preference.

READY-MADE FELT

Many of the projects based on flat felt can be made of felt bought from craft shops. I have been lucky enough to find naturally hand-dyed pure wool felt in sumptuous colors in stores local to me, and this can also be found online. One word of warning—industrial felting processes enable felt to be made from acrylic or wool/viscose mixtures, and you may find that this is what your local store stocks. Of course it is still usable but will not have the same intensity of color and tactile pleasure of pure wool felt.

WOOL TOPS

These are the raw materials that you use to make your own felt fabric, and there is a wide variety on the market. Most types of sheep's wool will felt successfully and you can buy fibers from other types of animals for felting. For ease of use and reliability I use merino wool tops, and most of the projects in the book are made from these. These fine wool fibers come in long lengths and are generally sold by weight. They are dyed in a spectacular array of colors and felt easily. The fineness of the fibers also means that they readily attach themselves to other fabrics and so work very well for nuno felting (see page 15). You may find that your local craft store stocks a range of wool tops, but, if not, search online for a good supplier.

FELT MADE FROM RECYCLED KNITTING

You may have discovered that placing an item of pure wool knitwear into a hot wash cycle produces a felted fabric that retains the flexibility of the knitted structure. When the fabric is cut it does not fray or unravel and so can be used for a range of projects, even taking the place of handmade or ready-made felt in some cases. It provides an excellent opportunity for recycling, especially as you may already have some sweaters that have suffered this unfortunate end by

△ **FELTS**
Clockwise from top left: Merino wool tops, felted knitwear, merino wool tops, commercial felt hand-dyed with natural dyes.

accident! Source suitable knitwear for felting in your own closet, from family and friends, as well as in thrift stores. Instructions for felting knitwear are on page 15.

Threads

For stitching and joining your pieces, as well as attaching findings such as brooch backs, I recommend polyester sewing thread as it is fine and can be easily hidden within the felt. It can be used doubled to create a stronger thread for stitching that needs to bear weight or be very firm. It is also fine enough to be used for stitching on beads.

To decorate your felt jewelry there is a wealth of hand- and machine-embroidery flosses available from craft stores, and Internet suppliers offer still more riches. My favorite thread for stitching onto felt is shiny, thick, viscose embroidery floss from India. I use it on the bobbin of the machine (see page 18), working on the back of the project, or double it and use it as hand-embroidery floss. Its beautiful luster shows up well against the matte surface of the felt. My other favorite thread is a wool/acrylic thread that again can be used on the bobbin of the machine or for hand embroidery.

▽ **THREADS**

Clockwise from top left: *Wool machine-embroidery flosses, Indian viscose embroidery flosses, polyester sewing thread.*

Fabrics

Various projects in this book require the use of other fabrics to form a base or decorative contrast to the felt. In some cases the type of fabric is very important in order for the felting process to work, as in the Rosy Nuno Scarf (see page 98), so do check the materials list for each project before you begin.

Ribbons and braids

These are useful not only for decoration but also as a means of attaching jewelry to the body. Again, these can come from a wide range of sources; try the Internet, craft stores, and vintage fairs.

▽ **RIBBONS**

Clockwise from top left: *Silk ribbon, polyester satin ribbon, vintage satin ribbon, ric-rac trim.*

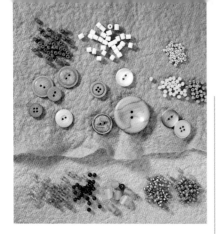

Buttons and beads

Buttons are a great way to add character to felt jewelry as their naïve charm fits perfectly with felt's simple aesthetic. I love to source these in a random way, raiding friends and family's button boxes and hunting in thrift stores and antique markets. There are so many kinds of buttons, but my favorites are vintage mother-of-pearl and Bakelite buttons. Choosing the buttons is a very exciting part of a project for me and selecting a harmonizing color combination is very satisfying.

Beads add texture and small accents of color. Again, there are many sizes, shapes, colors, and materials to choose from. It is worth buying ones you are particularly drawn to so that you always have a selection to choose from for a project.

△ **BUTTONS AND BEADS**

Top row: Large glass rocaille beads, bone beads, small glass rocaille beads.
Middle row: Plastic and Bakelite buttons, faceted glass beads.
Bottom row: Frosted glass beads of various shapes and sizes.

Findings

Many of the projects will need some way of attaching them to your body or clothing. A large range of findings can be found in craft stores and bead suppliers. If you are making jewelry from felt beads you will need to have something strong to thread them onto, such as cotton, linen, or silk thread. Tiger tail, a plastic-coated stainless steel wire, is very strong and is safely fixed using tiny metal beads called crimps. Transparent or colored jewelry elastic is a good option for bracelets.

Dissolvable film is transparent film that is generally used in machine embroidery to create lace-like fabrics, among other effects. In felt making it can be used to create a network of wool tops and stitches. This can then be placed in the washing machine on a hot wash to dissolve the film and felt the wool fibers (see Using Dissolvable Film, page 15), creating unusual structures and textures.

If you would like to color felt yourself or create tie-dye effects, commercial hot water dye can be used. Follow the instructions on the pack for wool and see also the section on health and safety when using dyes (see page 18).

▽ **FIXINGS**

Clockwise from top left: Tiger tail, crimps, bobby pins, ear wires, hair elastics, barrettes or hairclips, jewelry elastic, brooch backs, plastic headband, hot water dye, ring mount, dissolvable film

Felt-making equipment

Much of the equipment needed for felt making is easily found around your home, so you won't have to buy much. Check the individual lists for each project, as some of these items are specific to only a few pieces.

A towel is useful for providing friction and for absorbing and squeezing out excess water. Keep a stock of old towels especially for felt making. Bubble wrap also provides friction and helps to hold the water in the fibers being worked. Generally it is best to use the kind with smaller bubbles for the scale of felt in this book. You will need to replace it periodically as the bubbles pop and the bubble wrap becomes flattened. Recycling packaging is a good idea, and once your friends know that you have a use for bubble wrap, bundles of it will start to come your way.

Bowls or jugs are needed for water. An old squeeze detergent or shampoo bottle is helpful for distributing water over the surface of the fibers. Make sure the water you use initially in the felting process is around body temperature and not too hot.

Your choice of detergent could range from dishwashing liquid and shampoo, to olive oil soap and soap flakes I like to use a gentle ecological liquid detergent. You may also like to try olive oil soap—it is more difficult to apply to the fibers, but it is wonderfully kind to your skin. If you are doing a great deal of felt making or you find that you are allergic to detergents, lanolin, or wool, you may want to wear protective gloves. I prefer latex ones as they fit well, allowing a good grip on the materials and equipment. (Note that if you are using gloves to create friction during the wet flat felt process, these should be plastic, not latex.)

Fine netting is necessary to protect the fibers during the wetting and rubbing stages. Nylon tulle can be bought very cheaply and cut up into useful-sized pieces for samples, larger felts, and scarves. Another good option is to recycle old net curtains that you may have or can source from thrift stores. The netting used must be a synthetic fiber such as nylon, or you may find that it attaches itself to the felt you are making.

A length of dowel makes an excellent and versatile roller. It can be bought in various thicknesses and lengths according to your needs. For most purposes a length approx 20 in. (50 cm) long and $1\frac{1}{2}$ in. (4 cm) in diameter is perfect. You could also use a rolling pin, though you should reserve it only for felt making and not use it in cooking. Invest in longer lengths of dowel of varying thickness if you would like to progress to making large-scale pieces of felt, such as scarves and hangings.

▷ **FELT-MAKING EQUIPMENT**
Clockwise from top left: Bubble wrap, plastic bowl, dishwashing liquid, squeeze bottle, needle felting tool, sponge block with spare needle embedded, wooden dowel, olive oil soap, latex gloves, nylon netting.

ALTERNATIVE FELT-MAKING EQUIPMENT

There are some alternative felt-making methods in this book. Needle felting is becoming increasingly popular. For this you will need to obtain special barbed needles, a tool to hold them either singly or in groups, and a block of sponge to protect you and your work surface, as well as to facilitate the process. These are often sold in kits along with suitable wool fibers.

It is also possible to felt in your washing machine. I have a machine that allows me to select various cycles and temperatures so that I can have some control over the process. See page 16 for more advice on felting in the washing machine.

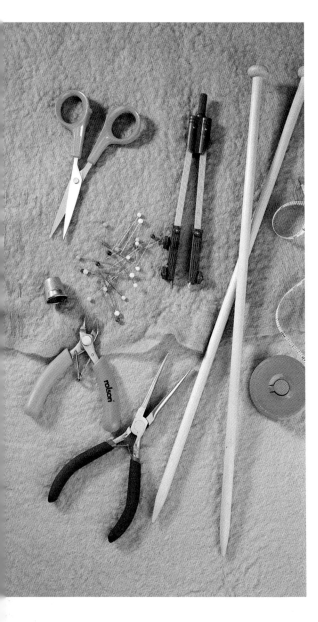

Sewing, knitting, and jewelry-making equipment

In order to decorate and construct your jewelry you will need a variety of other equipment. Check the individual lists for each project, as some of these items are specific to only a few pieces.

If you are adding small beads to your work, it's useful to have beading needles, which are very fine and have narrow eyes that will go through the smallest of beads. Embroidery needles have larger eyes to accommodate thick embroidery threads. Long darning needles have large eyes for accommodating strong threads or cords and are very useful for threading felt beads into necklaces and bracelets.

A good, sharp pair of embroidery scissors used only for fabric and threads will be invaluable for cutting out detailed pieces such as the Leaf Shadow Scarf (see page 84).

Glass-headed pins are useful when working with thick fabrics such as felt, as they tend to be longer and do not bury themselves in the surface. Quilting pins also work with felt as they have large flat heads.

A pair of compasses can be used to make circular templates for many of the projects. A tape measure is useful for some items that need to be accurately fitted to the wearer.

The Knitted Neck Warmer (see page 90) involves making felt yarn that is then knitted up. Large wooden knitting needles make this a tactile and speedy task. Fine metal knitting needles are useful for pushing through felt beads to make a threading hole.

Jewelry pliers will be needed to attach some of the findings. They are also very useful for pulling a needle through felt when threading up felt beads, unless you have already made a hole. You will also need flat pliers or a crimp tool to fasten crimps when using tiger tail. Wire cutters are required to cut tiger tail to length.

If you are sewing for long periods of time, a thimble will help to prevent your fingertips from getting sore. It is also useful for pushing needles through dense felt.

A sewing machine will help with stitching or constructing some projects, and if you have a free machine-embroidery function, you can add some sophisticated decorative effects to pieces made from flat felt, as well as construct felt using dissolvable film (see page 15).

◁ **KNITTING AND SEWING EQUIPMENT**
Clockwise from top left:: *Embroidery needles and beading needles (pushed into the felt), embroidery scissors, glass-headed pins, compasses, knitting needles, tape measure, flat-nosed pliers, wire cutters, thimble.*

techniques

Once you understand the basic principles behind felt making, you can explore the processes and experiment with new ways of working, developing your own unique style and aesthetic.

Traditionally, felt is made from animal fibers. All such fibers are covered in microscopic, overlapping scales called cuticles. Because of the unique construction of such fibers, when heat, moisture, and friction are applied through various means, the cuticles start to lift up, interlock, and then matt together, forming a strong bond. Adding some kind of soap or detergent aids this process further.

Felt can be made in many different ways, but the above principles always apply. This book explores a number of approaches across twenty-four projects. The felt-making processes are shown in individual projects, but here are summaries of each process.

Felt beads

One of the easiest things to do and a great place to start is to make a felt bead (see Beaded Felt Bracelet, page 20). Many shapes can be made using the basic process of sculpting with the pressure of your hands. The beads can be decorated with threads and colored tops during the felting process, as well as being embellished further with embroidery, beading, wrapping, cutting, and dyeing.

Once you have mastered beads, the next step is to try making other structures, such as rings and bangles (see African Bangles, page 40), ropes and tentacles. Again, these can be used as a basis for all kinds of stitched and beaded decorative techniques.

Flat felt

Many of the projects feature flat felt that has been cut, stitched, and manipulated into jewelry forms. The basic process is described in the Abstract Bangle project (see page 60) and, of course, can be scaled up to make larger items such as scarves (see Leaf Shadow Scarf, page 84), and still further if you would like to apply it to major pieces of work, such as hangings and throws. I suggest in many of the projects that you invest some time making larger pieces than you need for the project itself as it is very useful to have a ready supply of felt in a range of colors to use in different pieces of work.

Nuno felt

A good progression from flat felt is making nuno felt (see Rosy Nuno Scarf, page 98). This is where felt fibers are attached to fine, sheer fabrics, such as chiffon or muslin. The fibers creep through the tiny holes in the fabric and attach themselves, resulting in an exquisite fabric that has the texture of felt, yet is light and flexible. This makes it ideal for scarves and larger items such as garments. Combining different types of fabrics with the way the fibers are applied can result in many different exciting patterns and textures.

Adding patterning during the felting process

All three of the above processes can be further enhanced through the use of patterning with fibers and threads. These can be added in a number of ways during the felting process. It is important for these extra fibers to be incorporated during the dry construction process, as once the fibers become wet and begin to felt it is very difficult to introduce additional fibers.

Wool tops can be used to make painterly patterns on the felt (see Pebble Necklace, page 26). Add a final layer of tops arranged to form a pattern or design, or build color and pattern through the layers.

Wool yarns, such as knitting or tapestry wool, can be placed onto the layered wool tops. The fibers in the wool yarn will interlock with the wool tops and form a bond.

Fibers and threads such as silk tops and synthetic and embroidery flosses of various kinds can also be attached to felt pieces. In this case, as the structure of the individual fibers is very different, you will need to embed these into the structure of the felt. If you are using embroidery threads (see Rosy Nuno Scarf, page 98), you will need to place fine wisps of wool tops over the threads to bond the fibers in place.

Needle punched felt

This is becoming an increasingly popular way of making felt, as it is more transportable and no water or soap is needed (see Needle-punched Flower, page 102). This process is very versatile and can be used to produce sculptural shapes and add fine details, although I have shown only how to use it to attach fibers to layers of fabric.

Using dissolvable film

You may find that the above felt-making methods are not for you. It can require quite a lot of energy to make these pieces and if you have difficulties such as arthritis or back problems, you may be looking for an alternative way of making felt. One way is to sandwich wool tops between two layers of a special film that dissolves in water. The layers are sewn together on the sewing machine to produce a network of stitches that holds the fibers together (see Cloud Scarf, page 106). The fabric is then washed by machine to provide the heat, moisture, and friction necessary to felt the wool tops and, at the same time, dissolve the film. The disadvantages of this method are that the film can be expensive and the results unpredictable.

Felted knitting

Any knitting that is made from pure wool and has not been treated to make it machine washable can be felted in a hot wash in the washing machine, producing a fabric that has the texture of felt but retains the flexibility of knitted fabric. This is an alternative method of felt making that has some advantages: the fabric is already constructed and the washing machine does all the hard work. As knitting is time-consuming, an easy approach is to find pure wool knitwear that can be recycled—look in your closets and search thrift stores. The resulting fabric is used for projects such as the Phone or iPod Case (see page 116) and can also be used for many of the flat felt projects, such as the Dahlia Headdress (see page 72), the Fluted Corsage (see page 76), Bird Brooch (see page 94), or the Flower Brooch (see page 120).

HOW TO FELT KNITWEAR

It may be difficult to find knitwear that will felt successfully and it is very easy to over-felt the knitwear, resulting in fabric that is too thick to be used successfully. Follow these guidelines for effective washing machine felting.

Look at the fiber content label on the item and check that it is pure wool— look out for Shetland wool, lambswool, and cashmere in particular. Sometimes wool/nylon mixes will felt successfully, so these are worth trying. If the knitwear has been made from synthetic fiber, such as acrylic, it will not felt. Also, watch out for knitwear that has been treated to make it machine washable as it is unlikely to felt. Knitwear that advises you to "hand wash only" is most likely to be successful.

Place the knitwear in the washing machine. Add a gentle detergent and set the temperature to 140 degrees F (60 degrees C) if the sweater is Shetland yarn, 86 degrees F (30 degrees C) for lambswool. You may need to experiment with temperatures for other wool fibers. Set the cycle to one lasting about one hour and turn the machine on. When the cycle has finished, remove the knitwear from the washing machine and see whether the knitted fabric has felted. The individual stitches should have felted together and be no longer clearly visible and you should be able to cut the knitting without it unraveling. If this is not the case, try washing it again at a higher temperature. Leave the knitwear to dry in a warm place: if you use a tumble dryer, bear in mind that the knitwear may felt still further during drying.

Health and safety considerations for felt making

As with many creative practices, there are various hazards when making felt that may affect you. You may find that you have allergies to wool, lanolin (the natural oil in sheep's wool), or your choice of detergent, and if you are making felt on a regular basis, your hands can become very sore. For both of these reasons, I recommend that you wear protective latex gloves. If you are allergic to wool, I suggest you only make pieces that are not worn next to the skin, such as brooches and hair decorations.

Try different soaps such as olive oil soap, soap flakes, and gentle liquid detergents. Cheap detergents will wreck your hands more quickly and are not good for the environment, although there is a theory that these speed the felting process.

Take care of your back, hands, and wrists, as you will exert considerable pressure on all of these. People with carpel tunnel or arthritis may have particular problems. Consider other ways of felting, for example in the washing machine (see above) or needle felting (see page 15). You can also make flat felt (see page 13) with your feet by trampling and then rolling the felt on the floor instead of working it with your hands on a tabletop. Hold onto a tabletop or chair and stand on one foot, while rolling the felt with the other foot. You can also sit on a chair and roll the felt with both fee in front of you.

△ *There is a theory that cheap detergents will speed the felting process, although they will wreck your hands more quickly and are not good for the environment.*

decorating felt

Making the felt can be just the start of a project. Applying decoration of various types will lift your pieces to new levels of gorgeousness.

Stitching into felt

Felt is a joy to stitch into by hand or machine. The soft, thick, and forgiving nature of felt means that stitches you don't want to see can often be hidden within it. The needle can be passed invisibly through the layers and resurface where needed to make a stitch or attach a bead.

Knotted stitches

I often suggest finishing stitching with a knotted stitch to secure the end of the thread firmly. To do this, leave the threaded needle in the felt, wrap the thread around the needle twice and then pull the needle and thread through to make a firm knotted stitch. Repeat this as many times as you like to make sure your stitching will not come undone, or to make a long-lasting hold for jewelry findings such as brooch backs or barrettes.

Free machine embroidery

This is a very useful sewing machine function and can be used to create a great many effects. It is the nearest thing to drawing with stitch and allows maximum freedom of movement while stitching. Several projects in this book call for free machine embroidery, such as the Leaf Shadow Scarf (see page 84) and Cloud Scarf (see page 106). Check your manual to see if your sewing machine will do this form of embroidery or consult your supplier. It is referred to as "darning" in some machine manuals.

The feed dog is lowered and a special foot attached (usually it is shorter than a normal foot and is sprung), allowing the fabric to be moved in any direction. Have a go on scraps of felt to practice your technique before starting a project. Start by turning the wheel on the right-hand end of the machine to lower the needle into the fabric. Slowly press the foot control and once the machine has

started, move the fabric with your fingers, keeping them well away from the needle. As the feed dog is no longer there to guide the fabric, your hands now have control over the movement. Move slowly at first and then practice various lines and movements, such as swirls, to develop your skills. Once you have become confident, you can run the machine at a faster speed and move the felt at a corresponding rate. Adjustments may need to be made to the top or bobbin tension. If you find that the thread keeps breaking or is skipping stitches, try using a larger-sized needle. A common mistake is to forget to lower the presser foot and thereby not engage the top tension, resulting in loose, uneven stitching and possibly a thread jam under the needle plate.

Felt know-how

Do not machine stitch into damp or wet felt. Your sewing machine won't appreciate it and the inner workings may become rusty as a result.

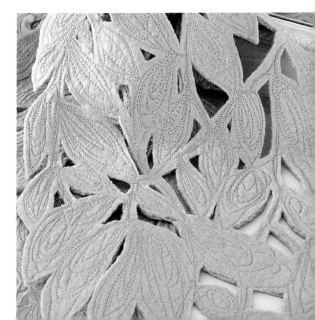

USING THICK THREADS ON THE BOBBIN

In many of the projects I suggest machine embroidery using a thicker thread in the bobbin and working with the back of the piece uppermost. A stronger, more luxurious line of stitching is made, depending on what kinds of threads are used. Viscose or rayon threads are commonly available and are used in these projects, but you may be able to find cotton and wool/acrylic threads too. If possible, wind the threads onto the bobbin in the normal way with your machine. If this is problematic, wind on by hand. Depending on the thickness of your thread, you may need to adjust the tension screw on your bobbin case to a looser setting. (Adjust the screw over a container since it if drops on the floor you may never find it again.) Test the stitching on some scrap fabric and adjust it again if necessary. Once you have started on your design, turn it over regularly to check it.

HEALTH AND SAFETY FOR FREE MACHINE EMBROIDERY

When doing free machine embroidery, you must be very careful not to get your fingers in the way of the needle. Standard practice is to use an embroidery hoop, which is safer and holds the fabric taut. However, felt is substantial enough not to need a hoop and in any case, you will find it difficult to fit the felt into one. This has safety considerations as an advantage of using a hoop is that it allows you to control the fabric by holding the hoop and so keeping your fingers out of the way of the needle. If you are embroidering without a hoop, concentrate on what you are doing and take great care not to stab your fingers.

Hand embroidery

The charming colors and naïve nature of felt means that it looks particularly great with hand-embroidery stitches. I love to go back to stitches learned in childhood, such as lazy daisy, cross stitch, and French knots. How to work these stitches is shown within the projects.

Health and safety for dyeing

Dyes can be very harmful if inhaled or absorbed through the skin. Make sure you wear a mask when dealing with dye in its dry powder form and wear protective rubber gloves throughout the process.

the projects

beaded felt bracelet

MATERIALS
- ¼–½oz (5–10g) of merino wool tops in each of orange, magenta, cherry, and fuchsia and approximately ½–¾oz (10–15g) of lime green
- Polyester sewing threads to match colors of wool tops
- Approximately 25 glass rocaille beads in toning colors for each bead
- 12 in. (30 cm) of clear jewelry elastic

EQUIPMENT
- Bowl of warm water
- Olive oil soap or liquid detergent
- Hot water for rinsing
- Towel
- Fine metal knitting needle (optional)
- Beading needle and a large darning needle
- Jewelry pliers (optional)

This project introduces you to making simple felt beads. From here you can go on to make beads of all shapes and sizes. They can be decorated in a number of ways including beading, embroidery, stitching on buttons, and tie-dyeing to make a variety of necklaces and bracelets, as well as other items such as earrings and rings. If you would like all the beads to be the same size (as in this project), it is best to prepare the dry stage of the beads all in one go.

Making the basic bead   1

1 Pull approximately 7 in. (18 cm) of wool tops from one of the rolls. When pulling off lengths of wool tops, place your hands well apart before pulling.

2 Divide the strip into two and use half a strip for the first stage. Tease this apart with your fingers to tangle the fibers together.

3 Roll the wool tops between the palms of your hands to form a rough ball.

2

3

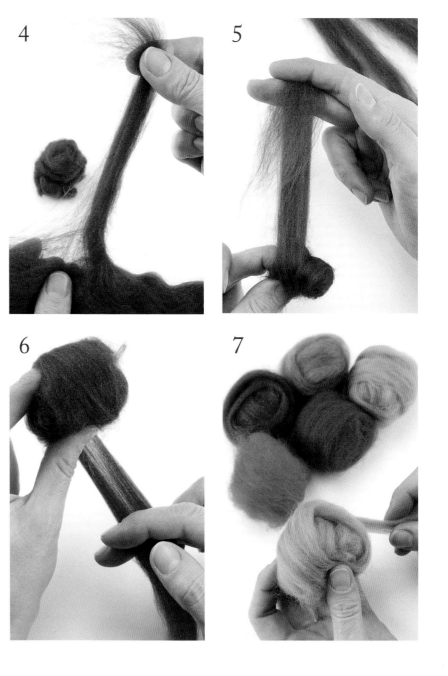

4 Take another strip of wool tops the same length as in Step 1. Divide the new strip and the remaining strip from Step 1 lengthways by pulling the fibers apart.

5 Wind the strips of wool tops around the rough ball in both directions. Winding tightly and firmly will produce a smooth finished bead with few wrinkles.

6 Continue winding the wool strips around the ball until it measures 2½ in. (6 cm) in diameter.

7 You will need six or seven beads in total, depending on your wrist size. Repeat Steps 1–6 with the other four colors of wool tops, making two green beads and one more in a color of your choice if necessary. As a guide, if your wrist measures 5½ in. (14 cm) you will need six beads and seven beads if your wrist measures 6¼ in. (16 cm).

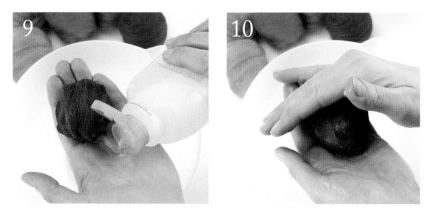

8   Dip a ball of wool tops into the bowl
     of warm water to soak it thoroughly.

9   Using olive oil soap or a drop of
     liquid detergent, work up a lather in
     the palms of your hands.

10   Coat the ball gently with the lather,
     smoothing down all the wool fibers
     with your hands.

11   Roll the ball gently in the palms of
     your hands for about a minute until
     the fibers start to felt. Then apply
     pressure as you roll the ball. Dip the
     bead into the water and apply more
     soap as necessary. Keep felting until
     the ball shrinks to approximately
     1¼ in. (3 cm) in diameter. It can take
     from 5 to 15 minutes to fully felt.
     Repeat the process with the rest of
     the balls.

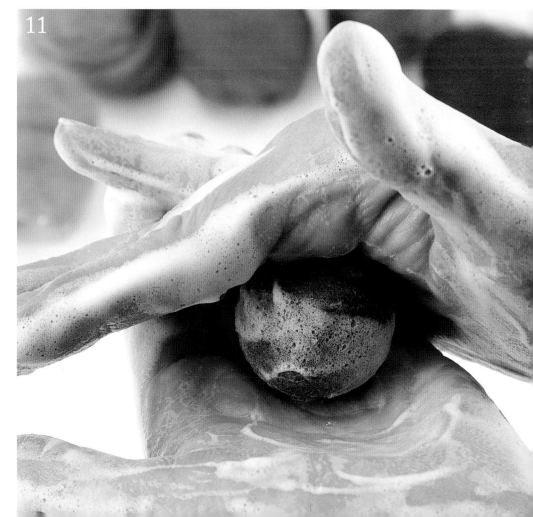

12

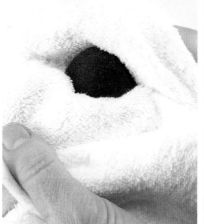

13

14

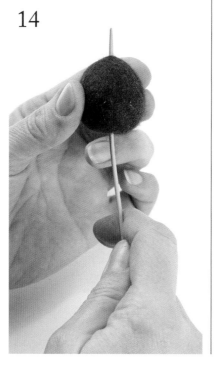

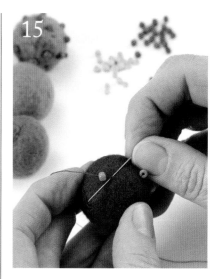

15

12 Rinse the bead by squeezing it thoroughly in fresh hot water to remove all traces of soap.

13 Squeeze the beads in a towel to speed up the drying process. Then reshape them with another quick roll in your hands.

14 If you wish, push a fine metal knitting needle through the center of each bead to allow the beads to be threaded more easily later on. Push several beads onto the needle, leaving a small space between each. Leave the beads to dry completely in a warm place.

Sewing on glass beads

15 Using doubled polyester sewing thread and a fine needle (or a beading needle if the beads have very small holes), stitch about 25 glass beads onto each felt ball. Make a very small backstitch underneath each bead. Then pass the needle through the felt to where you want the next bead. Make several knotted stitches (see Knotted Stitches, page 17) under the last bead.

16

Threading up

16 Line the felt beads up to make a good color mix. Thread the large darning needle with the jewelry elastic. Thread the beads on to the elastic. You may need pliers to help you pull the needle through the felt bead. Tie the ends of the elastic together in a knot. Repeat the knot two or three times to fasten securely.

△BERRY NECKLACE AND BROOCH

This berry necklace and brooch were made in the same way as the Beaded Felt Bracelet, but a selection of semi-precious beads such as garnet, amethyst, coral, and cornelian were used to embellish the balls. The brooch was made in the same way as the Button Flower Brooch (see page 36). Different-sized semi-precious beads were stitched on before adding a brooch back.

▷BEADED FELT NECKLACE

This vibrant necklace is made from a number of different-sized felt beads that have been decorated with buttons and beads in toning colors. The necklace is strung onto beaded tiger tail and fastened with crimps for a strong finish (see Pebble Necklace, page 26).

pebble necklace

MATERIALS
- ½–¾oz (10–15g) of merino wool tops in each of white, dark gray, and light gray
- A few wisps of black merino wool tops
- Length of jewelry wire, such as tiger tail
- Four crimps
- Magnetic fastening
- Approximately 40 ½ in. (1 cm) glass beads in a toning color, such as dark gray

EQUIPMENT
- Bowl of warm water
- Olive oil soap or liquid detergent
- Hot water for rinsing
- Towel
- Long darning needle
- Flat-nosed pliers
- Wire cutters

This beach-inspired project adds subtle patterning and stripes to felt beads using wool fibers to emulate the natural markings found on pebbles along the shoreline. All kinds of patterning can be applied in this way as part of the felting process and you may also wish to try applying pure wool yarns to similar effect. This project also shows how you can shape the beads with your hands once the felting process is underway, allowing naturalistic forms to be made. Choose complementary glass beads that are sympathetic to the theme, such as matte beads in a toning color.

Making the basic bead   1

1 Make a ball in each color of wool tops (see Steps 1–6 of Beaded Felt Bracelet, page 20), making them approximately 2³⁄₄ in. (7 cm), 3¹⁄₂ in. (9 cm), and 4¹⁄₂ in. (11 cm) in diameter.

2

4

2 Pull off thin strands of each color, including black, of wool tops and wrap them together around each ball to create the pebble markings. It is very important to apply the stripes at the dry stage, as it is very difficult to add them and felt them in once the felting process has begun.

3 Felt the beads (see Steps 8–14 of Beaded Felt Bracelet, page 20). In order to help the stripes felt effectively you can add extra soap to these areas. Halfway through the felting process, shape the beads into pebble shapes by squeezing and rolling them in the palms of your hands. Leave the beads to dry completely in a warm place.

3

Threading up

4 Measure around your neck and the area where you want the necklace to lie. Cut a length of jewelry wire about 4 in. (10 cm) longer than this and thread the darning needle with it. Arrange the pebbles in the order you want. Thread the first pebble onto the wire (you may need to use flat-nosed pliers to pull the needle and wire through the felt). Next add a glass bead. If the needle won't fit through the glass bead, remove it and thread a glass bead onto the wire by hand. Repeat this process until you have a glass bead between each ball.

5

6

5 Thread an equal number of glass beads onto the wire on either side of the felt pebbles until the necklace is the required length.

6 Thread the end of the wire through two crimps, through one half of the magnetic clasp then back through the crimps. Using the flat-nosed pliers, squash the crimps approximately $^{1}/_{4}$ in. (5mm) apart to fix the wire and clasp in place. Trim off any excess wire. Repeat for the second half of the magnetic clasp using the remaining two crimps.

folk art necklace

MATERIALS
- ½–¾oz (10–15g) of merino wool tops in each of dark gray, magenta, cherry, dark red, leaf green, and dark purple
- Toning rayon hand-embroidery flosses
- Polyester sewing threads to match colors of wool tops
- Approximately 27 small buttons in toning colors
- 40 in. (1 m) of narrow silk ribbon
- Strong jewelry thread or cord in a toning color

EQUIPMENT
- Bowl of warm water
- Olive oil soap or liquid detergent
- Hot water for rinsing
- Towel
- Fine metal knitting needle (optional)
- Hand-sewing, embroidery, and large darning needles
- Thimble
- Scissors
- Flat-nosed pliers (optional)

Felt is a joy to stitch into and this is particularly effective if you use a shiny rayon floss that contrasts well with the matte felt. Secure the ends of the flosses with tiny backstitches concealed within the felt. This necklace has a bohemian feel and has been decorated with a variety of hand stitches and tiny buttons. Go through your button box and choose the smallest that will tone beautifully with your chosen colors of wool tops. The piece is finished with a length of silk ribbon to tie around your neck.

Making the basic bead

1   Make nine balls of wool tops (see Steps 1–6 of Beaded Felt Bracelet, page 20), in a range of sizes approximately 2½ in. (6 cm), 3 in. (8 cm), 4 in. (10 cm), and 4¾ in. (12 cm) in diameter. Make one ball in each of dark gray, magenta, and cherry and two balls in each of dark purple, leaf green, and dark red. Felt the beads (see Steps 8–14 of Beaded Felt Bracelet). Allow them to dry thoroughly.

Decorating the beads

2 Using matching polyester sewing thread, hand stitch six or seven buttons onto the four largest beads, passing the needle and thread through the felt from one button to the position of the next.

3 Further decorate the same beads with cross-stitches using the rayon embroidery flosses and the embroidery needle. Make a firm backstitch behind one of the buttons, and then bring the floss up through the felt where you want the cross stitch to be. Take the needle back into the felt ½ in. (1 cm) in a diagonal line. Pass the needle through the felt, bringing it up ½ in. (1 cm) from the first two points.

4 Complete the cross-stitch by pulling the needle through and passing it back into the felt at a fourth point. Pass the needle through the felt to where you would like the next cross-stitch to be. When you need more floss, secure it with backstitches under a button. Embroider all the larger beads with cross-stitches.

5 Embroider the remaining five beads with star stitches and French knots. To make a star stitch, make two cross-stitches on top of each other to create an eight-pointed star.

6 Finish with two small stab stitches in the center of the star to hold the longer stitches in place.

7 To make French knots, bring the needle and floss through the felt. Wind the floss around the needle twice.

8 Take the needle back down into the felt, pulling the knot tight.

▽ FOLK ART EARRINGS AND RING

These earrings were made from two small white felt beads decorated all over with lazy daisy stitches, star stitches, stab stitches and French knots. The beads were then stitched onto ear wires using polyester sewing thread. The ring was made by slicing a gray felt ball in half using a craft knife. It was embroidered in the same way as the earrings, then fixed onto a ring mount with strong fabric glue.

Threading up

9 Arrange the beads in a pleasing composition of sizes and colors. Thread the long darning needle with the cord or strong thread and thread the beads onto it. Leave a length of cord at each end.

10 Make a loop at each end of the string of beads by looping the cord around your finger and then tying five or six firm half-hitch knots before trimming off the excess cord. Thread the silk ribbon through the loops and, once you have decided on length, tie the ends in a firm bow.

tie-dye necklace

MATERIALS
- Approximately 4oz (120g) of merino wool tops in white
- One pack of hot water multipurpose dye in navy and 1oz (30g) of salt for the dyeing process
- Elastic bands
- 40 in. (1 m) of strong jewelry thread or fine cord

EQUIPMENT
- Bowl of warm water
- Olive oil soap or liquid detergent
- Hot water for rinsing
- Towel
- Old saucepan for dyeing
- Rubber gloves for dyeing
- Large darning needle
- Flat-nosed pliers (optional)
- Scissors

Basic round felt beads can be shaped in many ways during the felting process by applying different amounts of pressure in various directions with your hands. Here, the tie-dyeing process has been used to create stripes. For simplicity, I have used a commercial hot water dye, but if you have skills in indigo dyeing why not apply them to this project? You could also try tie-dyeing some of the other projects in the book, such as the African Bangles (see page 40).

1 Make about 20 beads from the white wool tops (see Steps 1–14 of Beaded Felt Bracelet, page 20), using balls of wool tops about twice the size you want the finished bead to be. Once felting begins, roll in various directions to create a range of shapes. Select two thirds of the larger beads and wrap each one tightly with rubber bands.

1

2 Make the dye following the instructions on the pack and add all the beads to it. Simmer for ten minutes or follow pack instructions. Wearing rubber gloves, rinse the beads in warm water until the water runs clear. Squeeze in an old towel to absorb excess water. Remove the rubber bands. If beads are slightly misshapen, re-roll in your hands while damp. Leave to dry in a warm place.

3 Arrange the beads in the order you want them. Cut a length of strong thread approximately 4 in. (10 cm) longer than the necklace and thread the long darning needle with it. Push the needle through each bead, using flat-nosed pliers to pull it through if necessary. Tie the ends of the thread with several knots and trim.

2

3

button flower brooch

MATERIALS
- ½oz (15g) of merino wool tops in lilac
- 4-in. (10-cm) square of flat felt in duck-egg blue (see Steps 1–7 of Abstract Bangle, page 36)
- Three small buttons in toning colors
- Wool hand-embroidery flosses in greens, yellows, and purples
- Matching polyester sewing thread
- Brooch back finding

EQUIPMENT
- Bowl of warm water
- Olive oil soap or liquid detergent
- Hot water for rinsing
- Towel
- Embroidery and hand-sewing needles
- Thimble
- Template (see page 124)
- Stiff paper for template
- Pins
- Small, sharp scissors

Felt can be manipulated into a variety of shapes. This brooch project uses a simple oval pad made as an extension of the basic bead process. It is decorated with naive embroidery and buttons to make a charming brooch with a scalloped edge cut from flat felt.

Making the basic pad

1 Make a ball of lilac wool tops (see Steps 1–6 of Beaded Felt Bracelet, page 20), around 4 in. (10 cm) in diameter. Dip the ball into the warm water and begin to felt it (see Steps 8-11 of Beaded Felt Bracelet). When it begins to felt, shape it into a flat oval around 3 x 2½ in. (8 x 7 cm) by pressing gently between your hands while you continue to felt. Rinse thoroughly in hot water to remove soap. Squeeze the oval into a towel to absorb excess water and reshape it in your hands. Leave to dry in a warm place.

Embellishing the pad

2 Arrange the three buttons in position, towards the top of the oval pad. Stitch them on using the embroidery flosses or polyester sewing thread.

3 Using the green and light green embroidery flosses and embroidery needle, stitch a backstitch stem below each button. To work backstitch, bring the needle and floss up through the felt. Take a small stitch to the right, bringing needle up again a little to the left of where it first went in. Continue in this way to make a line of stitching.

4 Add green and light green leaves using detached chain stitch. To work detached chain stitch, bring the needle up through the felt. Take the needle in at the same point and out again a short distance away. Leaving the needle in position, bring the floss under the needle point and then pull the needle through to form a looped stitch.

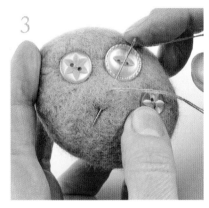

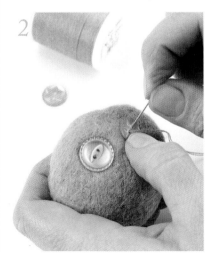

5

6

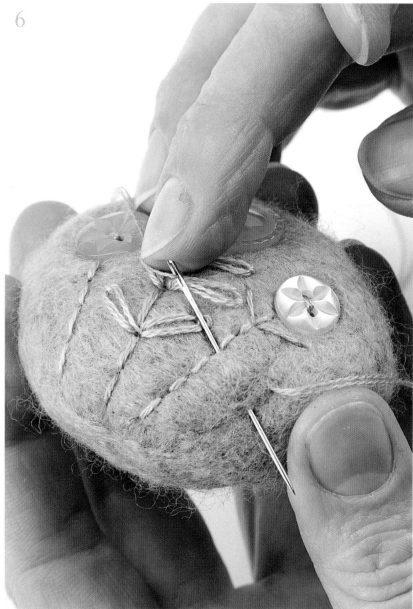

5 Complete the stitch by passing the needle back down through the felt, going over the end of the loop, to hold the loop in place.

6 Add more leaves and stems using stab stitch. To work stab stitch, take the needle through the felt and out again to make a mark with the floss. Decorate the background using star stitch and French knots (see Steps 5–8 of Folk Art Necklace, page 32).

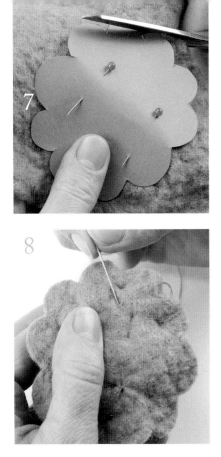

Making the backing

7 Trace the template for the backing onto the stiff paper. Pin it to the duck-egg blue felt and cut it out.

8 Center the oval pad on the backing and stitch the pieces together using backstitch (see Step 3). When making the stitches, take the needle through just the back of the oval pad rather than all the way through it.

9 Using polyester sewing thread, hand stitch on the brooch back finding.

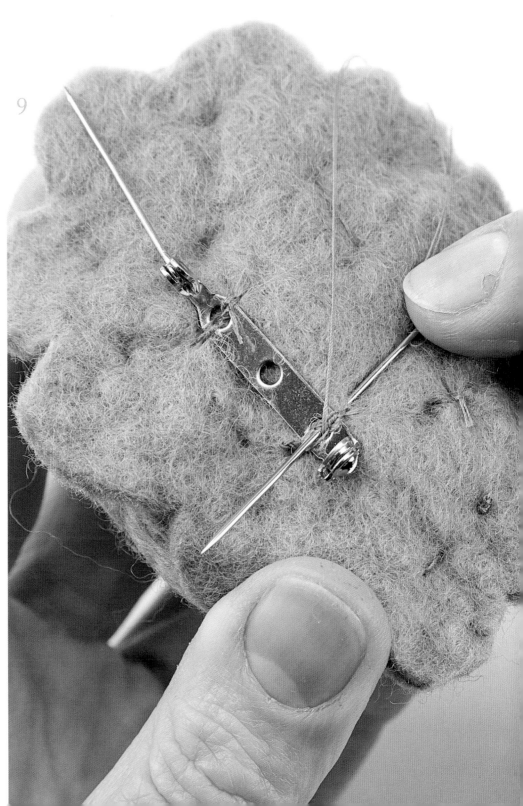

african bangles

MATERIALS
- 1oz (30g) of merino wool tops in each of white, ochre, burnt orange, dark gray, and black
- Polyester sewing threads to match colors of wool tops
- Approximately 40 white bone beads
- Approximately 35 buttons in white, ochre, orange, gray, and black
- Wool hand-embroidery flosses in ochre, burnt orange, and dark gray

EQUIPMENT
- Bowl of warm water
- Liquid detergent
- Hot water for rinsing
- Towel
- Sharp scissors
- Craft knife (optional)
- Hand-sewing, beading, and embroidery needles
- Thimble (optional)

This project features one basic technique that can be embellished in several ways to form a group of bangles. They can be worn singly or as an armful, inspired by the famous photographic portrait of Nancy Cunard in the 1920s. I have gone with an African aesthetic here, but the possibilities for embellishment are endless. You might like to embroider them with flowers, for example, as in the Folk Art Earrings (see page 33). You could also try adding pattern and color during the felting process, adding wisps of various-colored wool tops as you construct the bangle (see Pebble Necklace, page 26).

1

2

Making the basic bangle

1 Take a length of one color of wool tops long enough to wrap around the widest part of your hand twice. Entwine the length of wool tops together to make a twisted circle.

2 Take another length of wool tops the same color and size as the first and pull it into eight strips along its length (see Step 4 of Beaded Felt Bracelet, page 20). Use six of the strips to bind the circle as firmly and evenly as possible.

3 Apply a little detergent to the palm of your hand and create a lather. Wet the bound circle in the warm water, coat it in lather and rub gently with your hands, rotating along the length for several minutes to make sure that the fibers bond.

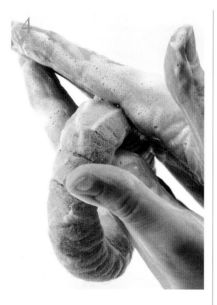

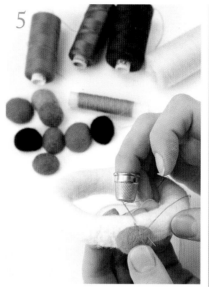

4 Rub the bangle, more firmly now, between the palms of your hands. Alternate this process with the rotational rubbing in the previous step and work your way around the circle several times until the bangle has shrunk to a size just big enough to slip over your hand. Rinse the bangle in hot water and squeeze out the excess water into a towel. Repeat Steps 1–4 with the remaining four colors of wool tops. Leave the bangles to dry in a warm place.

Bangle with felt balls

5 Make two beads measuring ¾ in. (2 cm) in diameter in dark gray wool tops and one each in ochre, burnt orange, and black (see Steps 1–14 of Beaded Felt Bracelet, page 20.) The balls need to be 40% bigger before felting. Cut each bead in half using scissors or a craft knife. Using matching colors of polyester sewing thread, hand stitch nine half beads onto the white bangle, using small oversewing stitches around each base.

Bangle with bone beads

6 Using black polyester sewing thread and the beading needle, stitch the bone beads onto the black bangle, making a small backstitch after each bead and passing the needle through to where you want the next bead to be on the bangle.

Felt know-how

One gray half bead will be left over—consider making it into an embroidered ring to complement the bangles (see Folk Art Ring, page 33).

Bangles with stitched embellishment

8 Using dark gray embroidery floss and the embroidery needle, decorate the burnt-orange bangle with cross stitches (see Steps 3–4 of Folk Art Necklace, page 30). Using ochre embroidery floss, decorate the dark gray bangle with a series of random-sized stab stitches (see Step 6 of Button Flower Brooch, page 36). Fill in the remaining spaces with burnt orange stab stitches.

Bangle with buttons

7 Using matching polyester sewing thread, hand stitch a random assortment of buttons onto the ochre bangle. When stitching on each button, pass the needle right through from front to back, making small invisible stitches on the inside of the bangle. Use several firm stitches for each button and then pass the needle through the felt to the next button position.

anemone ring

MATERIALS
- ¼oz (5g) of merino wool tops in each of duck-egg blue and green-gray
- Polyester sewing thread to match colors of wool tops
- Small turquoise, gray, and mauve glass beads

EQUIPMENT
- Bowl of warm water
- Olive oil soap or liquid detergent
- Hot water for rinsing
- Towel
- Scissors
- Hand-sewing and beading needles

This projects features two shaping methods. The first is a miniature version of a bangle (see African Bangles, page 40) to produce a ring. Practice making the ring, as the first attempt may be the wrong size. This basic ring shape could be developed in many ways with beads, embroidery, and attachments of various kinds such as felt flowers or felt balls, or take a look at the Tower Ring project (see page 64). The second method of shaping makes tiny tentacles of felt that could be adapted to other items, such as brooches and hair accessories.

Making the basic ring

1 Break off around 6 in. (15 cm) of duck-egg blue wool tops. Pull off a narrow strip long enough to wrap around your finger twice and entwine the length of wool tops together to form a circle.

1

2 Use the remaining strands to wrap
small wisps of wool tops around the
circle. Take some time to do this as
neatly and firmly as possible as this
will make the felting stages easier.

3

4

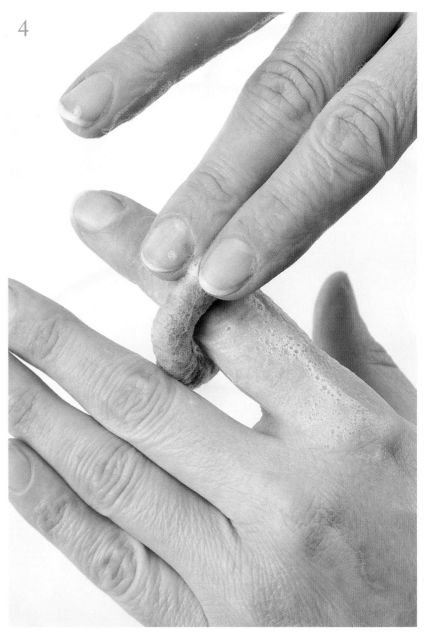

3 Dip the circle into warm water and
apply a small amount of detergent.
Gently massage the ring with your
fingertips, rotating it lengthways.
fingers, applying increasing pressure.

4 Rub the ring between your fingers,
applying increasing pressure. Stop
felting when the ring fits your finger.
Rinse in hot water and squeeze out
water with a towel. Leave the ring to
dry in a warm place.

5

6

Making the tentacles

5 Pull off lengths of duck-egg blue
wool tops around 4 in. (10 cm) long
and split them into five strands.
Repeat with the gray-green wool tops.
Taking one strand at a time, dip it in
warm water and apply a small amount
of detergent.

6 Rub each strand between the palms of
your hands until the fibers are felted
together and a pointed tentacle is
formed from each strand. Use a towel
to squeeze out the excess moisture and
leave the tentacles to dry in a warm
place.

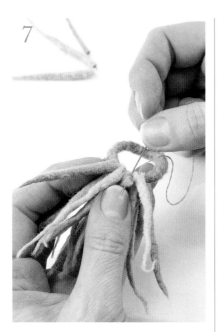

7 Cut the tentacles in half and trim each to 1½–2 in. (3–4 cm). Hand stitch them onto the ring base using polyester sewing thread to make small oversewing stitches. Apply them as closely together as possible to form an anemone shape.

Beading the ring

8 Using polyester sewing thread and the beading needle, stitch glass beads to the base of and between the tentacles. Make a firm backstitch in the felt after stitching on each bead. Then pass the needle through the felt to the next point at which you want a bead.

9 Continue to embellish the anemone by encrusting the sides of the base ring with beads, as well as attaching a few to the tentacles themselves.

Felt know-how

Using an artist's paint palette is a good way to keep your selection of beads together, and placing them on a piece of felt stops them rolling around.

Felt know-how

Consider making an anemone brooch by stitching the tentacles and beads onto a felt base and adding a brooch fastening to the back.

chunky necklace

MATERIALS
- 1oz (25g) of merino wool tops in six subtle shades of purple, green, and gray
- Polyester sewing threads to match colors of wool tops

EQUIPMENT
- Bowl of warm water
- Olive oil soap or liquid detergent
- Hot water for rinsing
- Towel
- Scissors
- Hand-sewing needle

This is an impressive piece that takes some investment in terms of time. The necklace is constructed from felt ropes and then thicker ropes are cut into chunks and stitched onto each necklace strand to make a highly textured piece of jewelry. Grouped together these necklaces make a real statement, but they can be easily adapted to your personal preference. If all six strands seem over-the-top, consider just making three. Just a single strand would work very well for many wearers.

Making the basic rope

1   Break off strands of wool tops between 39-48 in. (100-120 cm) long, one from each color, so that you end up with a variety of finished lengths. Split off half of each bunch of strands; the remaining strands will be used to make a thicker rope for the chunks.

2

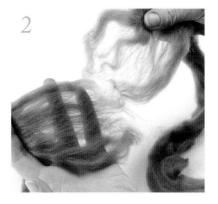

3

4

2 Tease and fan out each end of one strand with your fingers.

3 Place the ends together so that they integrate during the felting process to make a seamless circle.

4 Dip the circle into warm water and apply liquid detergent or soap to it. Rub the strands between your fingers until the two ends have felted together. Rotate and rub the rope in your hands to ensure that it is well felted and the join is invisible. (This may take from 20 minutes to half an hour for each rope.)

5 Repeat Steps 1–4 with the other colors of wool tops until you have six ropes of differing lengths. Fold each of the remaining six strands of wool tops in half before felting each one to form thicker ropes. Do not make them into circles. Rinse all the ropes in hot water, squeeze the excess water into a towel and leave all the ropes to dry completely in a warm place.

5

Applying the felt chunks

6 Using sharp scissors or the craft knife, cut the thicker felt ropes into small chunks measuring from ¼–½ in. (5mm–1 cm) long. Leave approximately 4 in. (10 cm) of one of the ropes intact for use in step 8.

7 Using the polyester sewing threads, hand sew each chunk onto the felt ropes with a single stitch, leaving an area of 4 in. (10 cm) undecorated on each rope.

Binding the necklace

8 Place the felt ropes together so that the undecorated spaces align. Use the spare felt rope to bind the ropes together. Hand stitch the binding firmly in place using polyester sewing thread.

Felt know-how

Consider using the ropes as a base for beading or for stitching on buttons and felt pieces to make other items such as necklaces and belts (see Layered Circle Belt, page 80).

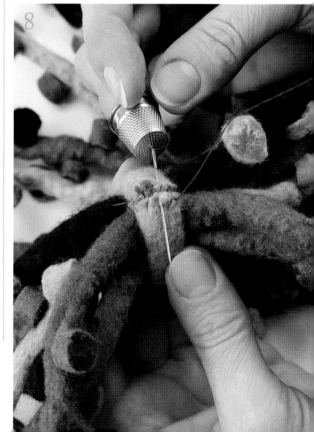

MATERIALS
- ½oz (15g) of merino wool tops in red and 1oz (30g) in pink
- Rayon hand-embroidery flosses in pink, orange, and green
- Small amount of polyester fiberfil
- Polyester sewing threads to match colors of wool tops
- Small button

EQUIPMENT
- Small piece of bubble wrap
- Plastic food wrap
- Bowl of warm water
- Olive oil soap or liquid detergent
- Hot water for rinsing
- Towel
- Sharp scissors
- Kitchen paper
- Embroidery and hand-sewing needles
- Template (see page 124)
- Stiff paper for template
- Pins
- Old knitting needle or similar

secret love locket

This three-dimensional hollow-form technique allows you to make a keeper for a sweetheart necklace. Romantically decorated with lazy daisy stitches, it is fastened with a button and loop. It hides an embroidered heart necklace made using other felt-making processes in this book. This project could be adapted to make a much smaller ball to make into a locket to be worn around your neck.

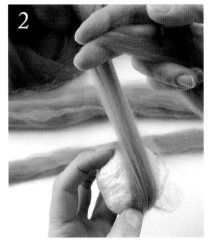

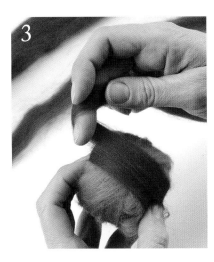

Making the ball

1 Make a ball of bubble wrap 2⅜ in. (6 cm) in diameter. Wrap the ball with plastic food wrap to give it a firm shape.

2 Divide a length of pink wool tops lengthways into four strips. Wind the strips around the bubble wrap ball in all directions to cover evenly. Reserve enough of the red and pink wool tops to make the flat felt and felt rope for the necklace.

3 Split the red wool tops into four strips lengthways. Wind these over the pink wool tops in all directions to cover the pink wool evenly.

4

5

6

4 Soak the ball in warm water, apply a little liquid detergent to the palms of your hands, and begin to felt the ball by rubbing it carefully with your hands. Apply increasing pressure until the ball has felted well, or about 10–15 minutes. Rinse the ball in hot water and squeeze excess water into a towel.

5 Using sharp scissors, cut the top third of the ball away, leaving a "hinge" of ⅝ in. (1.5 cm) joining the top and bottom sections.

6 Remove the bubble wrap ball and fill the felt ball with crumpled paper towels. Leave to dry in a warm place.

7

8

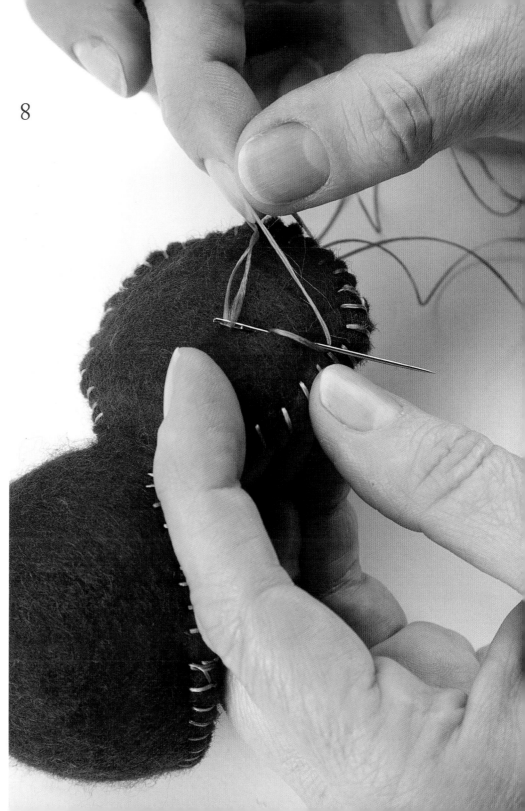

Embroidering the ball

7   Using green rayon embroidery floss
    and the embroidery needle, stitch
    around the cut edges of the ball with
    blanket stitch. To work blanket stitch,
    bring the needle through the felt and
    wrap the floss around the needle
    from right to left. Continue to pull
    the needle through the felt to
    complete the stitch.

8   Embroider the ball with lazy daisy
    flowers using pink and orange
    embroidery flosses. To make lazy
    daisies, bring the needle up through
    the felt where you would like the
    center of the flower to be. Take the
    needle in at the same point and out
    again a short distance away. Leaving
    the needle in position, bring the floss
    under the needle point and then
    pull the needle through to form a
    looped stitch.

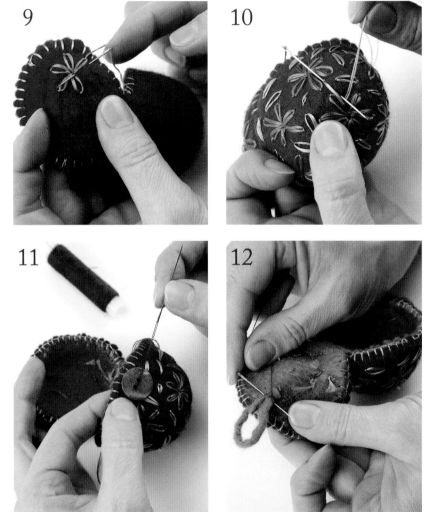

9 Take the needle back down through the felt, going over the end of the loop to hold the loop in place. Take the needle back to the center of the flower and repeat the stitch to form flowers with five or six petals.

10 Using detached chain stitch, embroider leaves in the remaining spaces. Detached chain stitch is just one segment of lazy daisy stitch (see Steps 4–5 of Button Flower Brooch, page 36).

11 Using polyester sewing thread, hand stitch the button onto the center front edge of the lower half of the ball.

12 Make a length of fine pink felt rope measuring 27–30 in. (70–80 cm) long and ¼ in. (7mm) in diameter (see Steps 1-4 of Chunky Necklace, page 50, but make a much finer rope and do not join the ends). Cut off a length 2½ in. (6 cm) long. Fold in half, and, first ensuring loop fits over button, stitch it to the center front underside of the lid above the button.

Felt know-how

You will only need a small amount of flat felt, so keep the remainder for another project, such as the Tower Ring (see page 64).

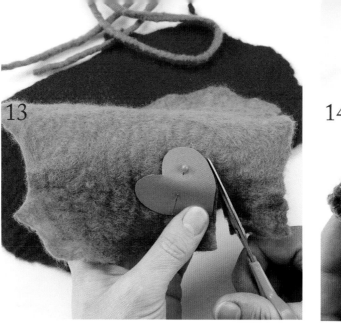

13

14

15

Making the necklace

13 Make two small pieces of flat felt using the remaining red and pink wool tops (see Steps 1–7 of Abstract Bangle page 60). Transfer the template onto stiff paper, then pin it onto the felt pieces and cut out one in each color.

14 Embroider the hearts with lazy daisy stitch (see Steps 8-9) and detached chain stitch (see Steps 4–5 of Button Flower Brooch, page 36). Join the hearts together using blanket stitch (see Step 7), leaving a small gap from the V of the hearts to the side for stuffing. Stuff with fiberfil, using the knitting needle to push it in, and close the gap with blanket stitch, leaving enough space at the top to push in ends of felt rope and enough thread to finish the next step.

15 Push the ends of the remaining felt rope into the gap. Secure the rope and close the gap with several firm stitches through the hearts and the felt rope. Place the heart necklace in the locket and fasten the button.

abstract bangle

MATERIALS
- Merino wool tops
- Machine-embroidery flosses or polyester sewing threads in three toning colors

EQUIPMENT
- An old towel
- Bubble wrap
- An old net curtain or tulle netting
- Squeeze bottle
- Warm water
- Olive oil soap or liquid detergent
- Plastic gloves or bags
- A rolling pin or piece of wooden dowel cut to desired length
- Bowl or other container for water
- Hot water for rinsing
- Template (see page 124)
- Stiff paper for template
- Scissors
- Pins
- Sewing machine

This project illustrates the basic process for making flat felt that is then cut, manipulated, and stitched to create jewelry. Use this process to make all sizes of felt, scaling up the equipment as appropriate. For very large pieces, lay the towels out on the floor and get your friends to help you felt, or try rolling with your feet when your hands and back get tired. This 1950s-inspired project is made from extra-thick felt that stiffens further once the decorative machine stitching has been applied.

1

2

Making flat felt

1 Lay the towel on the work surface and place the bubble wrap, bubble-side up, on top. Pull off short lengths of the wool tops approximately 4–6 in. (10–15 cm) long. Use the flat edge of your hand to create "sheets" of wool. Place these sheets onto the bubble wrap, overlapping each section and staying within the edges of the bubble wrap. Cover an area 50 percent larger than the size of the final piece.

2 Place another layer of wool tops onto the first one at right angles to it, maintaining even layers. For this bangle, you will need six layers, but for most purposes, three or four layers are fine. Apply each additional layer at right angles to the last.

3 Lay the netting flat over the wool tops. Fill the bottle with warm water and a squirt of liquid detergent if using. Squeeze soapy water over the surface of the netting. Make sure the fibers are completely soaked as any dry fibers will not felt. If using olive oil soap, make sure it penetrates through the netting to the fibers.

3

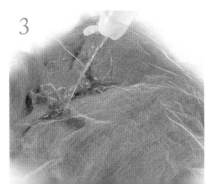

4 Put a plastic glove or bag over your hand to help your hand slide more easily. Rub your hand over the surface of the netting until the fibers are all wet and the netting has been flattened.

4

5 Rub gently for several minutes and then remove the netting. Carefully lift and turn the whole mat of fibers over, replace the netting, and rub the other side, adding more soap or liquid detergent if necessary. Remove the netting.

6 Wrap the fibers and the bubble wrap firmly around the rolling pin or wooden dowel and roll for a few minutes in one direction, applying firm, even pressure along the length of the rolling pin. Unroll and turn the felt 90 degrees before continuing to roll. Keep rolling for 10–15 minutes, changing the angle every few minutes. When the felt is matted and reduced in size, unroll it. (See Felt know-how, opposite.)

7 Squeeze some of the water and liquid detergent from the felt and rinse it in the hot water. Repeatedly throw the felt vigorously onto a hard surface to complete the process. The felt will rapidly shrink and bubble up slightly. Periodically dip the felt into the hot water to warm it up before throwing it down again. (If you don't want the felt to have a bubbly appearance, then continue rolling for several more minutes and omit the throwing stage of the process.) Squeeze water from the felt by laying it flat between dry towels and rolling over it with the dowel or rolling pin. Leave the piece of felt to dry completely in a warm place.

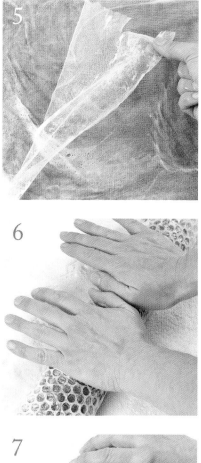

5

6

7

Making the bangle

8 Transfer the template onto stiff paper and cut it out. Ensure that the center circle will fit over your hand and adjust the size if necessary. Pin the template to the felt and cut it out.

9 Thread the sewing machine with a contrasting thread on the top spool and bobbin (See Using Thick Threads on the Bobbin, page 18). Stitch around the bangle in random lines with the first of your chosen colors.

10 Continue to stitch using the second and third colors, making a series of random overlapping lines around the bracelet. If the bangle is no longer flat, you can press it using a steam iron and damp cloth.

9

10

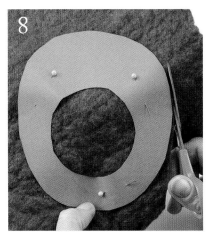

8

Felt know-how

Test to see if the felt is ready by pinching the surface with your fingers. If fibers come away readily then it needs more rolling. If they are firmly felted together, you are ready for the next stage, which is to throw it onto a hard surface. The length of time felting takes will depend on several things: the size and thickness of the felt, the type of fiber, and even your personal body weight and strength.I find that larger people find it easier and quicker to make felt than our petite friends! It will also depend on the end purpose of your felt so it is up to you decide when it is done. For jewelry, I recommend felting the pieces as hard as possible so that they wear well.

tower ring

MATERIALS
- Small amounts of merino wool tops in four shades of red and pink
- Polyester sewing thread to match one color of wool tops

EQUIPMENT
- An old towel
- Bubble wrap
- An old net curtain or tulle netting
- Squeeze bottle
- Warm water
- Olive oil soap or liquid detergent
- Plastic gloves or bags
- A rolling pin or piece of wooden dowel cut to desired length
- Bowl or other container for water
- Hot water for rinsing
- Pair of compasses
- Stiff paper for templates
- Pins
- Small embroidery scissors
- Long darning needle

This project brings together two felt-making processes, flat felt and a felt ring. The flat felt circles are cut in decreasing sizes to make a tower and are then stitched to the ring. Think about other shapes that could be cut from flat felt, such as flowers that could also be embroidered and beaded. Consider making them at the same time as this project, as you will have more than enough flat felt pieces to make several rings that could be worn together.

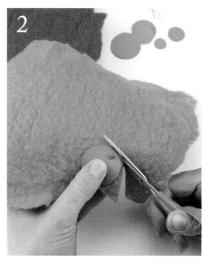

Making the tower

1 Make up small pieces of flat felt in varying colors (see Steps 1–7 of Abstract Bangle, page 60). Make a felt ring in a color of your choice (see Steps 1–4 of Anemone Ring, page 44).

2 Using the compasses, make six paper circles with the following radiuses: $\frac{1}{4}$ in. (0.5 cm), $\frac{3}{8}$ in. (1 cm), $\frac{1}{2}$ in. (1.2 cm), $\frac{5}{8}$ in. (1.4 cm), $\frac{6}{8}$ in. (1.7 cm), and $\frac{7}{8}$ in. (2 cm). Cut out the templates, pin them to contrasting colors of felt, and cut out felt circles using the small embroidery scissors.

3 Ensure that the colors vary with the increasing size of the templates so that the same colors are not next to each other on the ring. Stack the felt circles in order of size.

4 Thread the needle with polyester sewing thread. Bring the needle up through the felt circle tower and back down again, stitching the whole tower together. Repeat this several times. Using several oversewing stitches on each side of the ring base, stitch the tower firmly to the ring. Secure the thread using several knotted stitches (see Knotted Stitches, page 17).

3

4

MATERIALS

- Merino wool tops in pink, orange, lilac, blue, purple, duck-egg blue, and lime green. (I made pieces with (1¾oz) 50g of wool tops each, meaning I had plenty of felt left over for other projects.)
- Polyester sewing threads to match duck-egg blue wool tops
- Wool hand-embroidery floss in two shades of green
- Four small buttons plus one large button for fastening
- Small beads approximately ⅛ in. (4mm) across

EQUIPMENT

- An old towel
- Bubble wrap
- An old net curtain or tulle netting
- Squeeze bottle
- Warm water
- Olive oil soap or liquid detergent
- Plastic gloves or bags
- A rolling pin or piece of wooden dowel cut to desired length
- Bowl or other container for water
- Hot water for rinsing
- Pair of compasses
- Templates (see page 127)
- Stiff paper for templates
- Scissors
- Pins
- Sewing machine
- Hand-sewing, embroidery, and beading needles
- Thimble (optional)

flower bouquet neckpiece

Make and wear this spectacular piece for a spring party or celebration. The neckpiece is made from flat felt and character is added through embroidery and acid-bright beads to pick up on the color of the felt leaves. As you will be making flat pieces of felt in a variety of colors, you will have plenty over for other projects. This project could be interpreted in a number of ways to make different-sized neckpieces of varying complexity, as well as hairpieces, brooches, or even motifs to be stitched onto felt slippers.

1

Making the neckpiece base

1 Make a piece of felt in each color, using three layers of tops (see Steps 1–7 of Abstract Bangle, page 60). Transfer the four templates onto stiff paper and cut them out. Using the compasses, make five circular paper templates with the following radiuses: $\frac{1}{2}$ in. (1.2 cm), $\frac{7}{8}$ in. (2 cm), 1 in. (2.7 cm), $1\frac{1}{4}$ in. (3.2 cm) and $1\frac{1}{2}$ in. (3.7 cm).

2 Cut the neckpiece base template out of duck-egg blue felt. Using the sewing machine and polyester thread, stitch around the edges, approximately $\frac{1}{8}$ in. (4 mm) in. Add a buttonhole large enough for your button at one end of the narrow strip. If you don't have a button hole function on your sewing machine, cut a slit for your button and finish the edges with blanket stitch (see Step 7 of Secret Love Locket, page 54).

2

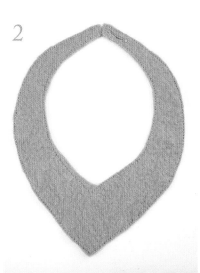

Making the leaves

3 Pin the leaf templates to green and duck-egg blue felt. Cut out seven large leaves and six small leaves.

4 Using backstitch (see Step 3 of Button Flower Brooch, page 36), the embroidery flosses, and the embroidery needle, create a central vein down each leaf.

5 Using stab stitch (see Step 6 of Button Flower Brooch), add side veins to each leaf.

Making the flowers

6 Use the paper circle templates to cut two 1½ in. (3.7 cm), one 1¼ in. (3.2 cm), one 1 in. (2.7 cm), two ⅞ in. (2 cm), and three ½ in. (1.2 cm) circles from pink, orange, blue, lilac, and purple felt. Using scissors, snip from the rim towards the middle all around one of each of the three largest circles to make daisy petals. Make the largest daisy by layering one 1½ in. (3.7 cm) circle on top of the other with two smaller circles on top. Pin the layers together. Repeat the layering process to make the two smaller daisies.

7 Using the templates, cut out three star flowers, one $1\frac{1}{2}$ in. (3.7 cm), two $\frac{7}{8}$ in. (2 cm), and three $\frac{1}{2}$ in. (1.2 cm) circles in different colors of felt. To make the largest flower, layer the $1\frac{1}{2}$ in. (3.7 cm) circle on the bottom, then a star flower, then a $\frac{1}{2}$ in. (1.2 cm) circle. Pin the layers together. Make two more flowers using a star and $\frac{1}{2}$ in. (1.2 cm) and $\frac{7}{8}$ in. (2 cm) circles.

8 To make the three circular flowers, use the templates to cut out one $1\frac{1}{2}$ in. (3.7 cm), one $1\frac{1}{4}$ in. (3.2 cm), three 1 in. (2.7 cm), three $\frac{7}{8}$ in. (2 cm), and three $\frac{1}{2}$ in. (1.2 cm) circles from different colors of felt. Use one circle of each size to build the largest flower. Use the remaining circles to build two smaller flowers. Pin the layers together.

Assembling the flowers

9 Arrange the pinned flowers into a necklace shape, ensuring that you have a good composition of sizes and colors.

10 Using the polyester sewing thread and hand-sewing needle, stitch a button into the center of four of the flowers, stitching through all the layers.

Embellishing the flowers

11 Using the polyester sewing thread and beading needle, stitch beads to the petals of the button flowers, pushing needle and thread through bead and all layers.

12 Use more beads to decorate the centers of all the remaining flowers, again stitching through all the layers.

13

▷**FLOWER BARRETTE AND BROOCH**
You can use the flower forms with leaves to make individual brooches and hair decorations. Stitch a barrette or brooch back finding onto the reverse.

14

Assembling the neckpiece

13 Arrange the leaves on the base and pin them in place. Hand stitch each leaf onto the base using polyester sewing thread

14 Arrange the flowers over the leaves. Pin and then stitch them in place. Stitch the large button to the end of the neckpiece base to align with the buttonhole.

MATERIALS

- Merino wool tops in five shades of coral, red, and magenta.(Make pieces using around 1¾oz (50g) of each color, and then you will have some leftover flat felt for other projects in this book.)
- Polyester sewing threads to match colors of wool tops
- Length of ribbon long enough to tie around head and make a bow.

EQUIPMENT

- An old towel
- Bubble wrap
- An old net curtain or tulle netting
- Squeeze bottle
- Warm water
- Olive oil soap or liquid detergent
- Plastic gloves or bags
- A rolling pin or piece of wooden dowel cut to desired length
- Bowl or other container for water
- Hot water for rinsing
- Templates (see page 125)
- Stiff paper for templates
- Small sharp scissors
- Pins
- Hand-sewing needle
- Thimble (optional)

dahlia headdress

Inspiration for this project came from looking at needlework books from the 1930s when there was a fashion for making all kinds of flowers from felt. This is an updated version, using chunky handmade felt that is cut and manipulated with gathering stitches to make plush dahlias. The deep-colored flowers are then attached to a ribbon to tie around the head, and are very much influenced by Frida Kahlo's amazing sense of style. Think about making the project for a winter wedding, either for the bride or attendants, in a range of coordinating colors.

Cutting the flowers

1 Make a piece of felt in each of the
five colors (see Steps 1–7 of Abstract
Bangle, page 60). Use three layers of
wool tops to make felt that is
substantial enough to be cut, but not
too thick to work with easily.

2 Transfer the templates onto stiff
paper and cut them out. Making sure
all the colors of felt are used, cut out
three shapes each for the large spiky
dahlia and the small spiky dahlia
(as indicated on page 125).

3 Cut two shapes in different colors to
make the rounded dahlia (as indicated
on page 125).

Assembling the flowers

4 Using doubled polyester sewing thread and the hand-sewing needle, work a running stitch around the inner circle of a flower shape. Pull the thread tight to gather up the flower and secure it firmly with a few knotted stitches (see Knotted Stitches, page 17). Gather up each flower shape in this way.

5 Take the biggest shape of the large spiky dahlia and push the next biggest into the middle of it. Then push the smallest one into the middle. Stitch the layers together, securing the thread with firm knotted stitches. Repeat the process to make the small spiky dahlia. Repeat again with two shapes to make the round dahlia.

Assembling the headdress

6 Arrange the dahlias centrally along the ribbon and stitch them on with oversewing stitches through the edge of the ribbon and into the back of each dahlia. Secure the thread with a few knotted stitches (see Knotted Stitches on page 17).

7 To finish, fold the end of the ribbon in half lengthways and cut a slant across it. When opened out, it will form a "V" shape. Repeat on the other end. Tie the ribbon around your head, tying the ends in a bow; you may find that you need some bobby pins to keep the headdress in place.

▷DAHLIA CORSAGE

A single flower of either size or type could be made into an accessory. Here, a corsage has been made by stitching a brooch back finding onto a large spiky dahlia.

fluted corsage

MATERIALS
- Commercial felt or fine hand-made felt in five colors
- Matching polyester sewing threads
- Brooch back finding

EQUIPMENT
- Templates (see page 126)
- Stiff paper for templates
- Scissors
- Pins
- Hand-sewing needle

This versatile project makes good use of commercial felt, which can be purchased in a variety of colors and qualities. For best results I suggest you buy pure wool felt: I was lucky enough to be able to get felt colored with natural plant dyes in vibrant tones that work beautifully together. However, commercial felt is often made from acrylic that has none of the charm of wool, so make sure you know what you are buying, especially if you are using a mail order service. You could also make this project using pieces of felted knitting or lightweight hand-made felts if you have pieces left over from other projects.

Making the flower

1 Enlarge the template, transfer it onto paper and cut it out. Pin it to the felt and cut one shape from each color.

Making the corsage

4 Twist the joined edge of the corsage to form an "S."

5 Stitch down the ends of the "S" so that a flat back is formed and the front is a full, rounded shape. Finish by stitching a brooch back finding onto the back of the corsage

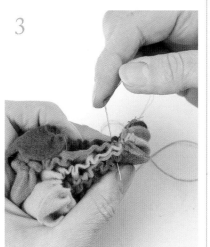

2 Using running stitch, stitch along the inside edge of each shape with matching thread. Gather the shape to form a ruffle and secure the end of the thread with several knotted stitches (see Knotted Stitches, page 17).

3 Place the five ruffled petals together with the gathered edges aligned. Oversew along the gathered edges.

▷ FLUTED FLOWER HAIR DECORATIONS

Making the bloom in a single color is also an option. Here, the larger flower was stitched onto a barrette to make a flamenco-style hairpiece. The cute miniature version was made from three pieces with three petals (see hairgrip template) and stitched onto a bobby pin.

layered circle belt

MATERIALS
- Merino wool tops in eight shades of purples, greens, and blues. (If you use approximately 1¾oz (50g) of each to make felt pieces, you will have enough leftover felt for other projects.)
- Approximately 14 buttons in toning shades
- Three buttons in three different sizes for the fastening
- Polyester sewing thread

EQUIPMENT
- An old towel
- Bubble wrap
- An old net curtain or tulle netting
- Squeeze bottle
- Warm water
- Olive oil soap or liquid detergent
- Plastic gloves or bags
- A rolling pin or piece of wooden dowel cut to desired length
- Bowl or other container for water
- Hot water for rinsing
- Pair of compasses
- Stiff paper for templates
- Pins
- Scissors
- Hand-sewing needle
- Thimble (optional)

Search through your button box to find buttons that will bring this piece to life. This belt features concentric layered circles cut from felt that have been fastened together through the centers with toning buttons and attached to a felt rope. The fastening is made from further layered buttons to echo the felt elements. You can choose what size to make the belt and whether you would like it to sit on your hips or lie snugly around your waist. The idea and process could also be adapted to make bracelets and hair decorations.

Making the felt

1 Make pieces of flat felt with each color of wool tops (see Steps 1–7 of Abstract Bangle, page 60). Use three layers of wool tops to make a felt that is substantial enough to be cut, but not too thick to work with.

2 Measure around your body where you would like the belt to sit. Use this measurement to determine how long to make the belt and how many circles you will need to cover it. Using a length of wool tops at least 60 in. (1.5 m) long (as it will shrink to about 48–52 in./ 1.2–1.3 m), make a felt rope (see Steps 1-4 of Chunky Necklace, page 50, but do not join the ends together). Leave the felt pieces to dry completely in a warm place.

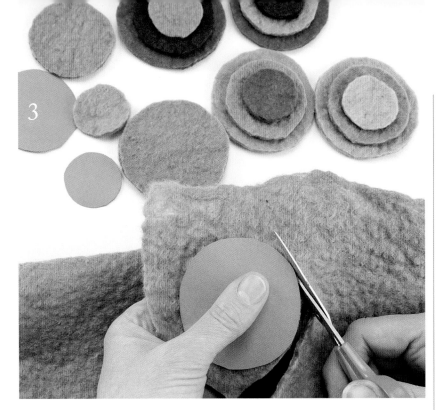

Making the layered circles

3 Using the compasses, make paper templates with 1³⁄₈ in. (3.5 cm), 1 in. (2.5 cm), and ³⁄₄ in. (1.7 cm) radiuses. Pin the templates onto the felts and cut approximately 14 circles of each size. Arranging the circles in concentric piles of the three sizes as you go will help you judge a good balance of colors across the belt.

4 Select a button for the center of each pile of three circles. Stitch the button to the center of each pile, stitching though all layers to join the pile together.

Assembling the belt

5 Arrange the circles in your desired composition. Starting 2 in. (5 cm) from one end of the felt rope, and attach the circles to your measured length. Working from the back and using small oversewing stitches, stitch each circle onto the rope. Once each circle is stitched on, pass the needle through the felt rope to the position of the next circle and stitch that in place.

Making the fastening

6 Once you have finished stitching on all the circles, trim the end of the rope, allowing an additional 2 in. (5 cm) as you did at the other end for the fastening.

7 Stack your three chosen buttons on top of one another and stitch them together onto the cut end of the rope to make a decorative fastening.

8 At the tapered end of the rope, cut a slit just longer than the diameter of the button for the buttonhole.

leaf shadow scarf

MATERIALS
- 10½ oz (300g) of gray-green merino wool tops
- Machine-embroidery flosses in leaf green and aqua

EQUIPMENT
- A few old towels measuring at least 80 in. (2 m) in length in total
- Bubble wrap at least 80 in. (2 m) long
- An old net curtain or other net at least 80 in. (2 m) in length
- Squeeze bottle or clean watering can
- Warm water
- Olive oil soap or liquid detergent
- Plastic gloves or bags
- A rolling pin or piece of wooden dowel at least 24 in. (60 cm) long
- Large bowl for water
- Hot water for rinsing
- Templates (see page 125)
- Access to photocopier
- Masking tape
- Craft knife
- Cutting mat
- Pins
- Small, sharp-pointed scissors
- Sewing machine with free machine function

The inspiration for this delicate scarf came from a photograph of a clematis vine through a conservatory roof at the Guggenheim Museum in Venice. This is a time-consuming project but well worth it in terms of impact. If you are new to using thicker threads on the bobbin, as well as free machine embroidery, I suggest that you make some practice samples first to get used to the process before embarking on the larger piece. A normal machine-embroidery floss was used on the top spool of the sewing machine, but thicker flosses were used on the bobbin for a more pronounced stitch (see Free Machine Embroidery, page 17 and Using Thick Threads on the Bobbin, page 18).

Getting the right thickness of felt is crucial, as if it is too thin it will buckle as you stitch. Too thick, and your machine foot will struggle to move over the surface comfortably. The felt will also need to be made well enough to hold together when cut into. The scarf may take up to an hour to felt, as it is quite a large piece. Its size means you will also need a large work surface, so consider using a floor space or even your backyard paving if you do not have a suitable worktop.

Making the felt

1 Cover an area of work surface at least 80 in. (2 m) in length with towels. Place the bubble wrap, bubble side up, over the surface. Place a layer of wool tops over the bubble wrap to form an area 80 x 20 in. (2 m x 50 cm). The scarf will shrink by about 40 percent, so it will need to be oversized at this stage. Instructions for felting such a large piece are given here, but refer also to Steps 1–7 of Abstract Bangle (see page 60).

2 You will need four layers of wool tops for the scarf, each placed at right angles to the last layer.

3 Lay the length of netting curtain over the entire surface of the wool tops.

4 You will probably need to fill a squeeze bottle several times over so using a watering can saves time on this project. Fill your container and add a small squirt of liquid detergent and squirt or sprinkle the water over the netting, making sure the whole length of wool tops is saturated. If you are using soap, rub it over the entire surface of the netting.

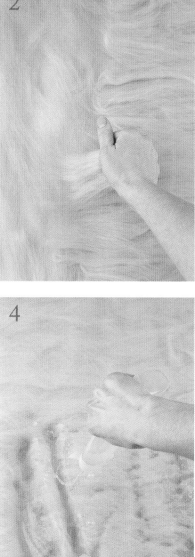

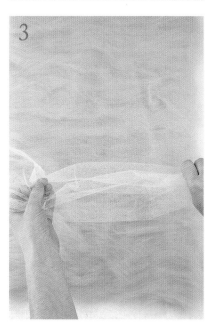

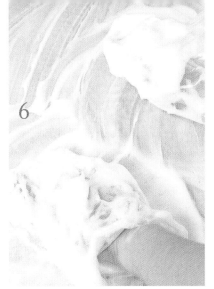

5 Put your hands in the plastic bags and rub the surface vigorously for five to ten minutes until the fibers start to felt. A friend can help you here, as it is a large surface area to rub. Avoid rubbing too much or the netting may felt to the wool fibers. Lifting and replacing the netting every so often will ensure that this does not happen.

6 Remove the netting and carefully turn over the felt. Replace the netting over the surface and continue to rub again for five to ten minutes.

7 Remove the netting completely. Place the rolling pin or dowel at one end of the scarf, aligning it with the width, and roll up the felt for about half the length of the scarf. Roll the felt in the usual way.

8 Repeat Step 6 on the other end of the scarf. Also roll the scarf up so that the dowel aligns with the length and felt it in the opposite direction. Again, do

this in segments unless you have a length of dowel that is the entire length of your scarf. Rinse the scarf in hot water and throw it onto the bubble wrap surface until it is well felted and has shrunk by approximately 40 percent; it should measure about 48 in. (120 cm) long. Ensure it does not shrink below this length or you will not be able to accommodate the templates. Use a towel to squeeze excess water from the felt and leave it to dry completely in a warm place.

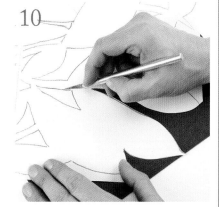

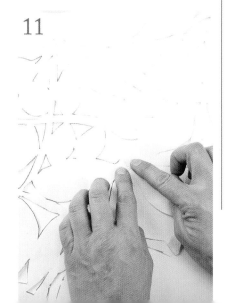

Making the templates

9 Make two copies of each template on a piece of paper at least 12 x 13 in. (30 x 33 cm). Using masking tape, join one set together at the middle to make one half of the scarf. Repeat for the second set of templates.

10 Place one template on a cutting mat. Using the craft knife, carefully cut away the spaces around the leaf shapes. Repeat for the second template.

11 Turn over one of the templates so that it forms a mirror image of the first. Align the ends of the templates and join them with masking tape to form the full length of the scarf.

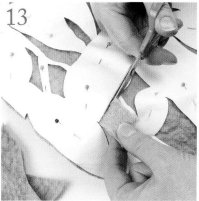

Cutting out the design

12 Lay the felt on a flat surface and pin the templates to it. Use enough pins to hold the templates securely, as this will help with accurate cutting.

13 Using the small scissors, cut around and between the templates. Take great care not to cut through any of the strands that hold the scarf together. Remove the template and all the pins.

Embroidering the scarf

14 Thread the machine with rayon machine-embroidery floss on the top spool of the machine. If you choose, you can use a thicker embroidery floss on the bobbin of the machine. This will mean that the right side of the scarf will be underneath and you will be working with the back uppermost (See Free Machine Embroidery, page 17). Set the machine to the free machine-embroidery function and use a free machine-embroidery foot. Embroider with swirling motions onto the leaves and in lines along the stems. Take care not to embroider too much at this stage if you are going to use a second color of floss.

15 Complete the scarf by embroidering over the surface again with the same techniques using a second color of embroidery floss.

MATERIALS
- 7oz (200g) in total of merino wool tops in white, black, red, and gray
- Black polyester sewing thread
- Machine-embroidery floss (optional)

EQUIPMENT
- An old towel
- Bubble wrap
- An old net curtain or tulle netting
- Squeeze bottle
- Warm water
- Olive oil soap or liquid detergent
- Plastic gloves or bags
- A rolling pin or piece of wooden dowel cut to desired length
- Bowl or other container for water
- Hot water for rinsing
- Scissors
- Sewing machine
- US size 11 (8mm) knitting needles
- Hand-sewing needle

knitted neck warmer

To make this project, patterned flat felt has been stitched and cut into a continuous strip to form an interesting and original yarn. It was then rapidly knitted up on large needles into a neck warmer that has a cute felt button fastener. I made the felt in several pieces to make it easy to handle in terms of space, but you could make one very large piece of felt if you have the space and tenacity.

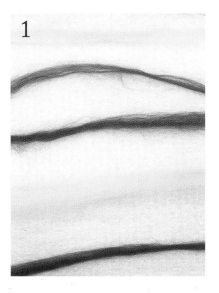

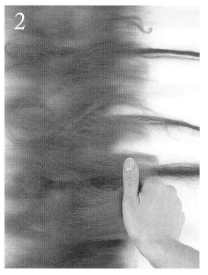

Making the felt

1 Make a piece of flat felt (see Steps 1–7 of Abstract Bangle, page 60). Lay out the towel on the work surface and cover it with the bubble wrap, bubble side up. Pull off fine strips of white and red wool tops 24 in. (60 cm) long and lay them out at random intervals on the bubble wrap.

2 Pull short tufts from the gray wool tops and lay them over the red and white strips, running in the same direction.

3 Half way across the width of the red and white wool tops, change the top layer to black wool tops.

4

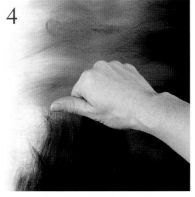

5

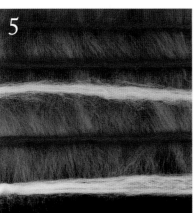

4   Cover the layer of black and gray wool tops with a second layer running at right angles, graduating from black to gray.

5   Lay out thin strips of red and white wool tops in stripes at right angles to the layer made in Step 4. Felt the wool tops into flat felt. Repeat Steps 1–5 to make four more pieces of the same felt. Leave the felt to dry completely in a warm place.

Making the button

6   Make a ball 3½ in. (9 cm) in diameter from red wool tops (see Steps 1–6 of Beaded Felt Necklace, page 20) and felt it to make a flat felt bead around 2½ in. (6 cm) across (see Step 1 of Button Flower Brooch, page 36). This will form the button on the neck warmer.

Making the yarn

7   Thread your sewing machine with sewing thread or embroidery floss. Stitch a continuous line of straight stitch up and down the pieces of felt, turning 180 degrees every time you get to the edge to stitch in the opposite direction. The lines of stitches should be no more than ³⁄₈ in. (1 cm) apart: use the edge of the sewing machine foot as a rough guide, running it along one line of stitching while you work the next one.

8   Cut the felt pieces into a continuous strip ³⁄₈ in. (1 cm) wide, cutting between the stitch lines and stopping ³⁄₈ in. (1 cm) short of the edges where you turned to stitch back in the opposite direction. Be careful not to cut through any of the lines of stitching. Roll the strips into balls of yarn.

6

7

8

9

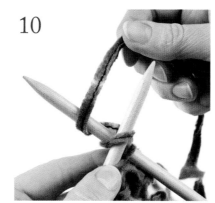

10

11

Finishing the neck warmer

12 Wrap the warmer around your neck to determine where to place the felt button. Stitch the felt button onto the scarf and push it through the loopy knitting to fasten the neck warmer.

12

Knitting the neck warmer

9 Using the US size 11 (8mm) knitting needles, cast on 12 stitches.

10 Knit the neck warmer using spider stitch. Work a row of knit stitch. On the second row, work a row of spider stitch by inserting the right-hand needle into the first stitch. Wind the yarn counter-clockwise around the tips of both needles, then around the tip of the right-hand needle only.

11 Pull the right-hand needle back and take the yarn through to create a new stitch that will be much longer than those in the last row. Slip the old stitch off the left-hand needle. Continue along the row in this way. Work alternate rows of knit stitch and spider stitch until you have a strip of knitted fabric approximately 48 in. (120 cm) long. Bind off.

MATERIALS

- ¾oz (15g) of merino wool tops in each of black, gray, and taupe
- Embroidery flosses in white, gray, and black
- Polyester fiberfil
- Polyester sewing thread (optional)
- Brooch back finding

EQUIPMENT

- An old towel
- Bubble wrap
- An old net curtain or tulle netting
- Squeeze bottle
- Warm water
- Olive oil soap or liquid detergent
- Plastic gloves or bags
- A rolling pin or piece of wooden dowel cut to desired length
- Bowl or other container for water
- Hot water for rinsing
- Templates (see page 126)
- Stiff paper for template
- Scissors
- Pins
- Embroidery needle
- Fine knitting needle

bird brooch

Soft grays and browns feature in this folk art-inspired bird brooch. The felt has been made to graduate in color, giving a naturalistic look. The brooch pieces have been decorated with naïve stab stitch and French knots before being joined together with blanket stitch. This project could easily be made from commercial felt if you would like to speed up the process and not make your own felt. Also consider making it in bright colors and adding sequins and beads to add some sparkle and create a completely different look.

Making the felt

1 Make a piece of felt with the wool tops (see Steps 1–7 of Abstract Bangle, page 60). Lay down a layer of black wool tops to cover an area around 14 in. (35 cm) square. Cover this with a layer of taupe wool tops at right angles to the first layer. Add a third layer at right angles to the second, graduating the color by laying gray over a third of the area, taupe over the next third, and black over the rest. This will make a piece of felt 10 in. (25 cm) square. Felt then leave in a warm place to dry.

Cutting the bird

2   Transfer the templates for the bird and wing onto stiff paper. Pin the bird template to the felt, positioning it to make best use of the graduated color. Cut out two bird shapes. Pin the wing template to the felt and cut out one wing.

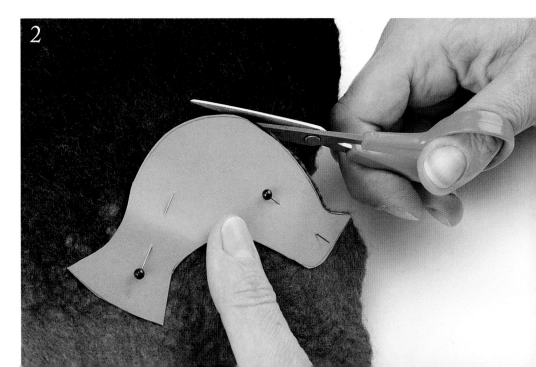

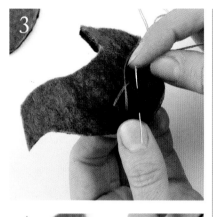

Embroidering the bird

3 Using long stab stitches (see Step 6 of Button Flower Brooch, page 36), gray embroidery floss, and the embroidery needle, decorate the lower part of the bird's breast and the wing.

4 Go over the breast and wing again with more stab stitches in black and then white embroidery flosses.

5 Add small dots to the bird's upper breast using French knots (see Step 6 of Folk Art Necklace, page 30) in gray and white embroidery flosses. Create an eye with a single French knot in black floss.

Assembling the bird

6 Using black embroidery floss, work blanket stitch (see Step 7 of Secret Love Locket, page 54) around the edge of the bird's wing.

7 Place the two bird shapes wrong sides together. Work around edges using blanket stitch in black embroidery floss. Stop stitching, leaving a small gap, but do not secure or cut the floss.

8 Stuff the bird with polyester fiberfil, pushing it through the gap and into the smallest areas using a knitting needle.

9 Continue the blanket stitch to close the gap and secure the floss with several knotted stitches (see Knotted Stitches, page 17).

10 Place the wing in position on the bird and stitch it in place with black embroidery floss by adding several more stab stitches through the wing and then through the bird to the back. Secure the floss with several knotted stitches.

11 Stitch the brooch back finding onto the back of the bird using embroidery floss or polyester sewing thread.

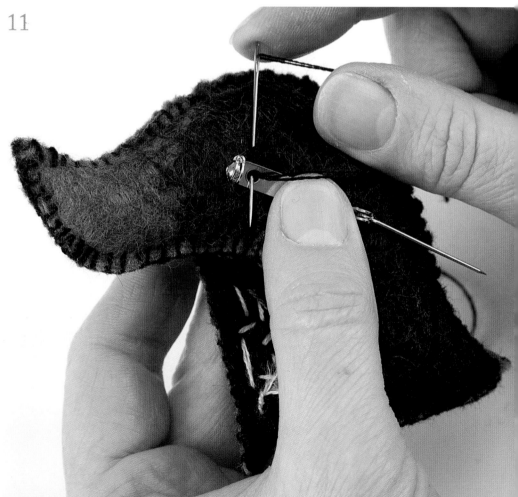

MATERIALS

- 80 x 20 in. (2 m x 50 cm) length of viscose or silk chiffon in pink
- Up to 3½oz (100g) in total of merino wool tops in three shades of pink and coral and two shades of green
- Viscose embroidery flosses in toning colors

EQUIPMENT

- One or two old towels measuring more than 80 in. (2 m) in length in total
- Bubble wrap measuring more than 80 in. (2 m) in length
- An old net curtain or other netting measuring more than 80 in. (2 m) in length
- Warm water
- Olive oil soap or liquid detergent
- Squeeze bottle or small watering can
- Plastic bags
- Large bowl for water
- Hot water

rosy nuno scarf

Nuno is a felt-making technique where fine layers of wool tops are attached to sheer fabric through the felting process. As the wool fibers shrink and contract the fabric puckers, creating a wonderfully textured and lightweight fabric that drapes well and is ideal for garments and scarves. This scarf features viscose embroidery flosses that add extra texture and detail. The choice of fabric is very important. It must be fine, translucent, and slightly rough to the feel. Fine silk chiffon is ideal, as are cotton muslins and scrims. My favorite fabric for this technique is viscose chiffon.

I suggest that you make a sample of nuno felt before starting the project to be sure your chosen fabric will react well to the process. It will allow you to get used to the process as well as gauge the amount of wool tops needed for the scarf to be a good weight. Making the scarf could take up to two hours, but small samples will be much quicker, allowing you to try out various ideas and color ways.

Laying out the design

1 Tear the selvages off the length of
chiffon so that it has a tattered edge.
Lay out towels with the bubble wrap
on top of them to make a working
surface measuring more than
80 x 20 in. (2 m x 50 cm). Lay the
chiffon flat on the bubble wrap.

1

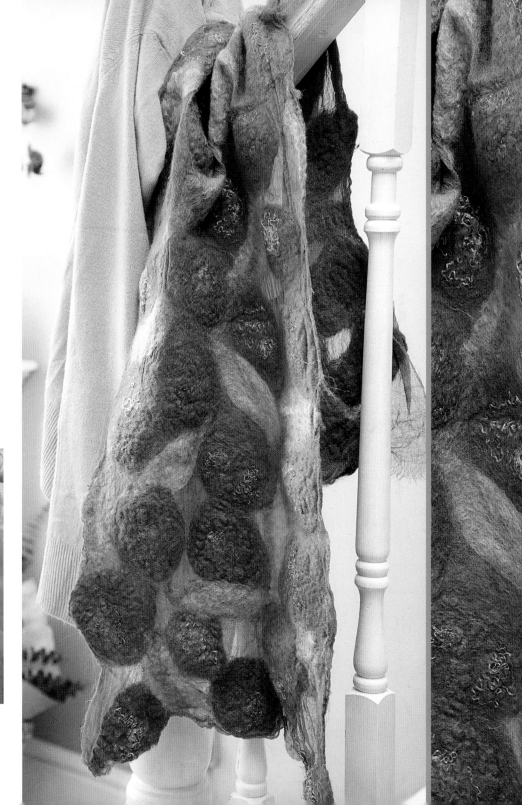

2 To form the roses, pull off wisps of wool tops in pinks and corals. Form the wool tops into rounds and lay them on the surface of the chiffon. Add further wisps of a contrasting color over the top of each round. Be sparing with the amount of wool tops so that the finished scarf is lightweight.

3 Take lengths of viscose flosses, form them into rough bundles and lay one over the top of each rose shape.

4 Pull off very fine wisps of wool tops and lay these over the viscose flosses. These will bond to the wool fibers beneath and help the viscose flosses attach to the felt.

5 To form leaves, pull off approximately 4–5 in. (10–12 cm) lengths of wool tops and divide them into about five strands. Form each strand into a leaf shape by pulling it apart in the center. Place leaves on the chiffon between the roses. Add a single strand of another color of green wool tops down the center of each leaf. Ensure that you leave gaps between roses and leaves so that the chiffon fabric is visible.

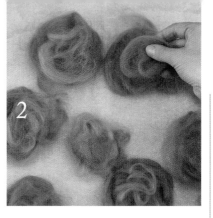

Felting the scarf

6 Lay the length of netting flat over the whole surface.

7 Squirt or sprinkle warm soapy water with the squeeze bottle or watering can through the netting and over the wool tops.

8 Place your hands in the plastic bags and rub over the surface of the netting. Ensure that the wool tops and the chiffon are completely wet.

9 Keep rubbing with the plastic bags until the wool tops start to felt.

10 After about 15 minutes, carefully turn over the scarf and rub the chiffon side with bubble wrap, encouraging wool fibers to creep through the holes in the fabric. If you pinch the chiffon you should be able to feel wool fibers coming through. Continue to felt and rub both sides of scarf alternately until the wool tops are felted and securely attached.

11 Rinse the scarf well in hot water to remove the soap and heat the scarf. Repeatedly throw the scarf onto the bubble wrap. This will cause the felt to shrink rapidly and the chiffon will wrinkle beautifully. Keep throwing until you are happy with the result. Squeeze the scarf in a towel to absorb excess water and leave it to dry completely in a warm place.

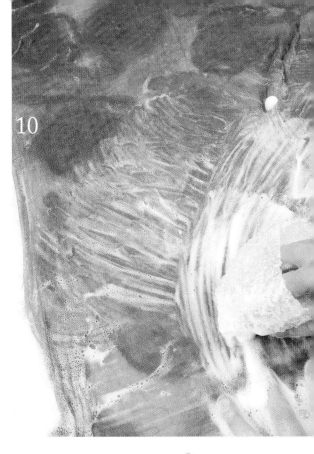

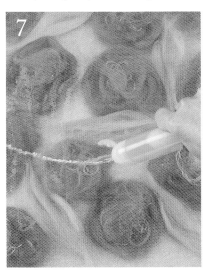

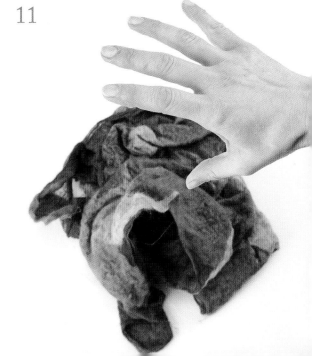

needle-punched flower

MATERIALS
- Small pieces of cotton organdy in mulberry red, pale pink, and pale green
- Small amount of merino wool tops in a toning color
- Polyester sewing threads to match colors of wool tops
- Glass beads in toning colors
- Brooch back finding

EQUIPMENT
- Needle felting tool
- Block of sponge foam
- Small, sharp scissors
- Beading and hand-sewing needles

In this increasingly popular felt-making technique, instead of water and soap being used to matte the fibers together, barbed needles are used to push them together. Tools that hold several barbed needles can be obtained from stores or websites specializing in felt making and craft materials. It is also possible to buy a machine called an embellisher that does the same task. It looks like a sewing machine except that there are no threads and the needle pad pushes the layers of fabric and wool tops together very rapidly and efficiently. Both techniques offer a wealth of possibilities, but here is a taster of what can be done.

These simple layered flowers in soft, flattering colors have been made with a needle punch tool then with toning glass beads. They can be made in three sizes and worn as a dramatic group, or used singly as corsages, hair accessories, shoe, or slipper decorations.

Making the organdy flower

1 For one flower, cut one 5½ in. (14 cm) square of organdy in mulberry red, one 4½ in. (11 cm) square in pale pink, and one 3½ in. (9 cm) square in pale green.

2 Following the template instructions on page 127, fold each of the squares into sixteenths, cut out a petal shape as shown, and unfold to make flowers.

Felting the flower center

3 Lay the flowers on top of each other in order of size. Pull off two small tufts of wool tops. Place one tuft over the other at right angles so that the fibers cross.

4 Form the wool tops into a small, round cushion by folding under the ends of the wool tops. Place this in the center of the layered organdy flower.

5 Place the flower on the sponge block. Using the needle-felting tool, push the needles repeatedly through the wool tops and organdy flower. Be careful not to stab your fingers.

6 Continue pushing the needles through the wool tops and organdy until all the layers of the flower are joined together and the wool felted.

7

Decorating the flower

7 Using the beading needle and
polyester sewing thread, stitch small
glass beads onto the felted center of
the flower.

Finishing the flower

8 Using the sewing needle and polyester
sewing thread, stitch a brooch back
finding onto the back of the flower.

9 To give a natural form to the flower,
crumple it in your hands to crease the
petals.

8

9

cloud scarf

MATERIALS
- 2½–3½oz (75–100g) of off-white merino wool tops
- Matching machine-embroidery flosses. (I used a thick viscose floss on the bobbin.)
- Polyester sewing thread in a matching color
- Approximately 125 different-sized mother-of-pearl buttons
- 80 x 32 in. (2 m x 80 cm) of heavy- or medium-weight dissolvable film

EQUIPMENT
- Pins
- Sewing machine, preferably with a free machine-embroidery function
- Washing machine
- Liquid detergent
- Hand-sewing needle

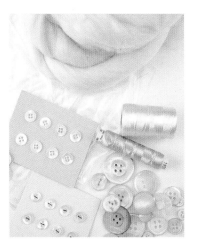

If you are finding the usual felt-making processes all rather exhausting, you may like to try some alternative methods of felt making. This scarf has been made by creating a network of wool tops and embroidery stitches sandwiched between two sheets of a special material called dissolvable film. I have used free machine embroidery for the stitching, but if you do not have this function on your machine you can experiment with other stitches, such as straight stitch and zigzag stitch. The wool and film sandwich is then put in the washing machine where the water will dissolve the film and, together with the heat and friction, will felt the wool fibers together.

Laying out the design

1 Fold the dissolvable film lengthways down the center and crease it with your fingers to make a visible center line. On a dry work surface, open the dissolvable film out flat. Pull off wisps of wool tops and lay them in swirls on the dissolvable film, laying them along the entire length but only on one side of the center line. It is important not to use too many wool tops in the construction in order to keep the fabric lightweight.

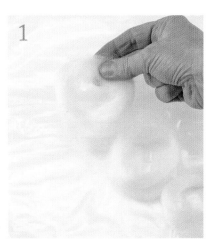

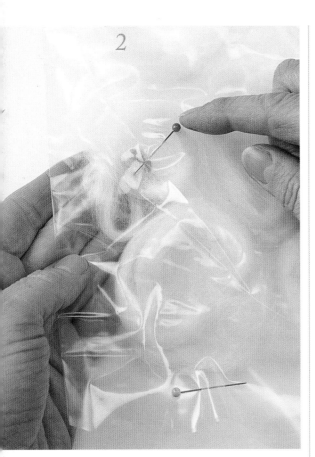

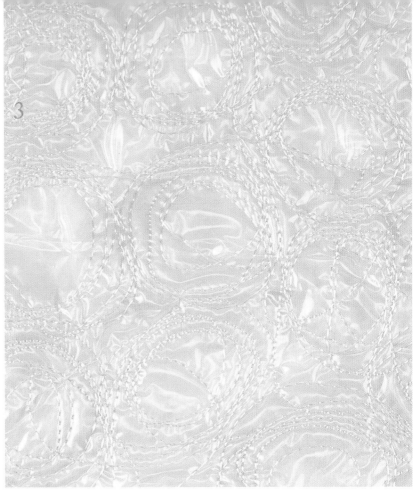

2 Fold the bare half of the dissolvable film over the wool tops. Align the edges of the film and pin them carefully together.

Embroidering the design

3 Thread the machine with off-white embroidery floss and set it to the free machine-embroidery function (see Free Machine Embroidery, page 17). If you choose, you can use a thicker floss on the bobbin (see Using Thick Threads on the Bobbin, page 18). Free machine embroider swirls forming a loose grid over the whole surface of the film and wool sandwich, removing the pins as you go. Embroider over the surface again, going over each swirl six or seven times in a random fashion to form a network of interconnecting stitches across the film. Make sure that each set of swirls interconnects with the next so that the finished fabric holds together well.

Felting the scarf

4 Put a small amount of powder or
   liquid into the detergent drawer of the
   washing machine. Place the fabric
   into the washing machine and set it to
   wash at 86 degrees F (30 degrees C)
   for 30 minutes. Once the washing
   cycle is complete, remove the fabric
   from the machine and leave it to dry
   completely. The washing machine
   should have dissolved the fabric and
   felted the wool, shrinking it by about
   one-third and leaving a cloud-like
   structure.

Embellishing the scarf

5 Using the polyester sewing thread,
   hand stitch mother-of-pearl buttons
   randomly over the surface of the scarf.

Sea-life head band

This mermaid-inspired hair decoration is made using the same dissolvable film process as the Cloud Scarf (see page 106). The anemone- and coral-like pieces are further embellished with beads and then attached to a plastic head band that has been covered in felt.

The same process could be used to produce sea-life creatures or flowers for corsages, hair barrettes, and neckpieces. The process for covering a ready-made item such as a head band is a useful one to master and can also be used to cover other bought jewelry items, such as bracelets.

MATERIALS
- Small amounts of merino wool tops in greens, turquoises, and blues. (You will need a little more of one of the green colors to cover the head band.)
- Plastic head band
- 12, 8 in. (20 cm) square pieces of heavy- or medium-weight dissolvable film
- Machine-embroidery flosses in blues and turquoises
- Polyester thread in a matching color
- Assortment of large glass beads in toning colors
- Small glass beads in turquoise

EQUIPMENT
- Bowl
- Warm water
- Liquid detergent
- Hot water
- Towel
- Pins
- Sewing machine with free machine-embroidery function
- Washing machine
- Powder or liquid detergent
- Scissors
- Hand-sewing and beading needles
- Thimble (optional)

Covering the head band

1 Pull off fine, long strips of green wool tops. Wind the wool tops around the plastic head band, ensuring it is fully covered with several thin layers.

2 Fill the bowl with warm water and dip the head band into it to saturate it. Apply a small amount of liquid detergent to the palm of your hand and rub the wool tops gently from side to side until fibers start to felt.

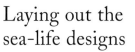

3 Rub the felt more vigorously between your hands and occasionally warm the head band up by dipping it into the water. When the wool tops are fully felted around the head band, rinse it in hot water and remove excess water by squeezing the head band in a towel. Leave it in a warm place to dry completely.

Laying out the sea-life designs

4 Lay a square of dissolvable film on a dry surface (even a small drop of water will spoil the film). Using blue and turquoise wool tops, pull off eight fine wisps of wool tops approximately 6 in. (15 cm) long. Twist the individual strands with your fingers.

5 Lay the eight strands onto the square of dissolvable film, crossing them over at the center to make a star with 16 points.

6 Place a second square of film over the wool tops and pin the squares together. Repeat Steps 4-6 twice to make a total of three stars sandwiched in film.

Embroidering the designs

7 Thread the sewing machine with blue embroidery flosses (see Using Thick Threads on the Bobbin, page 18). Free machine embroider (see Free Machine Embroidery, page 17) over the surface of the film using long stitches up and down the arms of the stars. Embroider the middle of each star using a circular motion.

8 Place several wisps of pale green and turquoise wool tops in an irregular circle on the center of a square of dissolvable film. Cover the wool tops with another square of film and pin them together. Repeat twice to make three pieces.

9 Thread the sewing machine with turquoise embroidery flosses. Free machine embroider with a circular motion over the surface of the film to make a network of stitches around and over the edge of the circle of wool tops.

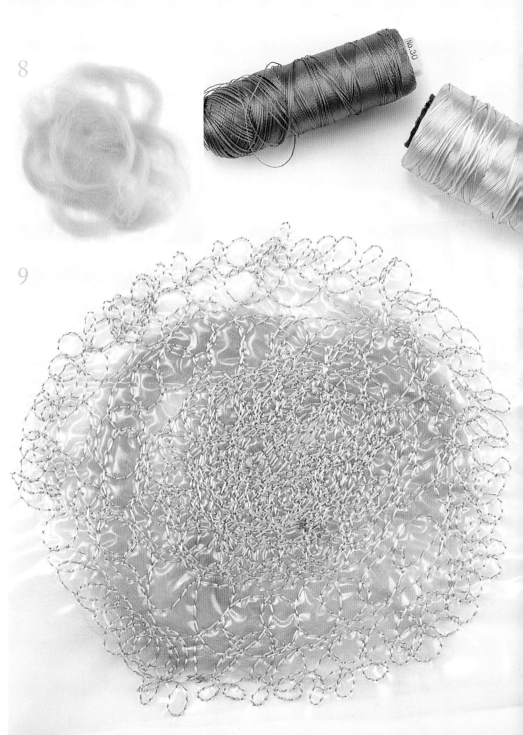

Felting the designs

10 Place the embroidered pieces in a washing machine for 30 minutes at 86 degrees F (30 degrees C) with detergent. This will felt the wool and dissolve the film at the same time. Remove and reshape the star pieces by teasing the arms apart with your fingers. Leave the felt pieces in a warm place to dry completely. `

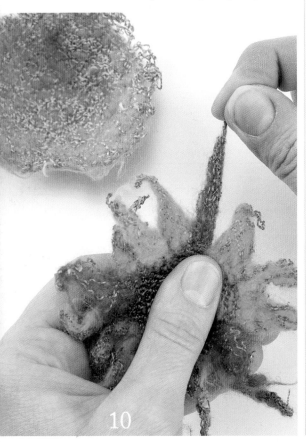

Assembling the sea-life pieces

11 Place each star on top of a circular piece of felt and hand stitch the two layers together.

Decorating the sea-life pieces

12 Stitch an assortment of large glass beads to each star. Use a small backstitch between each bead to hold it in place. Stitch on small glass beads between and around the large beads.

Assembling the head band

13 From the back, hand stitch the stars onto the head band. Make small oversewing stitches into the back of each star and through the felt covering the band.

phone or ipod case

MATERIALS
- Felted sweater or cardigan (see Felted Knitting, page 15)
- Selection of small pieces of vintage fabrics
- Hand-embroidery flosses
- Polyester sewing thread
- Selection of old buttons of various sizes and designs
- 8 in. (20 cm) of rick-rack
- 30 in. (80 cm) of ribbon or cord

EQUIPMENT
- Stiff paper to make template
- Pins
- Scissors
- Embroidery and hand-sewing needles
- Thimble (optional)
- Steam iron and cotton pressing cloth

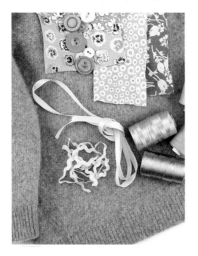

This appealing and useful accessory is made from a recycled sweater and other materials all sourced from thrift and antique stores. The application of retro fabrics and braids, hand-embroidery stitches, and buttons gives it a deliciously vintage feel.

Cutting out the case

1   Make a 4 x 5 in. (10 x 12 cm) rectangular template from stiff paper. Fold the bottom ribbed edge of the sweater so that you have a double thickness of ribbing. Pin the template to it so that the shorter edge aligns with the ribbing and the longer edge aligns with the fold. Cut around the other sides of the template. Remove the template and open out the felt so that you have a piece that measures 8 x 5 in. (20 x 12 cm).

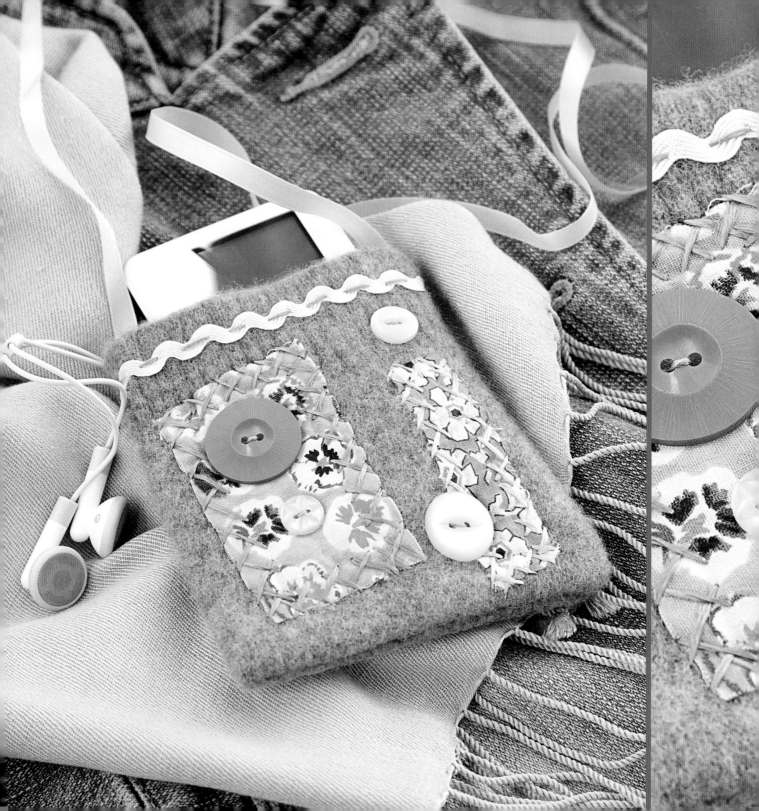

Decorating the case

2 Cut small scraps of fabrics and arrange them on what will be the front and back of the case (either side of the original fold), leaving a space in the center where the felt will be re-folded. Pin the fabrics in place once you are happy with the composition.

3 Using hand-embroidery floss, the embroidery needle, and herringbone stitch, appliqué the fabric onto the felt. To work herringbone stitch, determine two parallel lines, one on the felt just above the fabric, the other on the fabric, about ½ in. (1 cm) down from the edge. Make a small stitch from right to left on the upper line. Take the needle down to the lower line, a little to the right, and make another stitch. Continue stitching in this way, moving between upper and lower lines.

4 Pin the rick-rack approximately ½ in. (1 cm) away from ribbed edge of the felt. Hand stitch the rick-rack in place.

5 Using polyester sewing thread, hand stitch the buttons onto the fabric and background felt.

Finishing the case

6   Fold the felt in half, right sides together, and pin it along the side and bottom. Leave the ribbed edge open to form the top of the case. Using polyester sewing thread, backstitch (see Step 3 of Button Flower Brooch, page 36) around the edges, approximately ¼ in. (5 mm) from the edge. If you have used the end of a sleeve, turn it inside out and backstitch along the bottom.

7   Turn the case right side out and press it with the steam iron, using a cotton cloth to protect the embroidery. Stitch the ribbon or cord to the top inside corners of the case.

flower brooch

MATERIALS
- A red and a green felted sweater (see Felted Knitting, page 15)
- Small piece of lightweight dotted or patterned vintage fabric, such as crêpe
- Polyester sewing thread
- Five vintage buttons of various sizes
- Brooch back finding

EQUIPMENT
- Pair of compasses
- Templates (see page 126)
- Stiff paper for templates
- Scissors
- Pins
- Hand-sewing needle
- Thimble (optional)

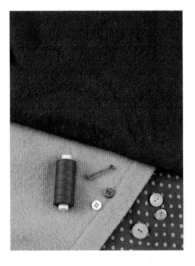

This project offers another excellent opportunity to recycle and source materials, such as knitwear and buttons, from thrift and antique stores: the cheerful dotted fabric was a must-buy from a vintage fashion fair. You won't use all the fabric from the felted knitwear so you could make a number of items, including the Phone or iPod Case (see page 116). I suggest you also try making some of the other projects from this book using felted knitting instead of flat hand-made felt. The Fluted Corsage (see page 76) and the Dahlia Headdress (see page 72) would work very well.

Cutting out the elements

1   1 Use the compasses to make a circular template with a 3 in. (7.5 cm) radius on stiff paper. Transfer the templates for the flower and leaf onto stiff paper. Cut out the templates.

2 Pin the flower template onto the red felted sweater and cut it out. Pin the leaf template onto the green felted sweater and cut out two leaves.

3 Place the circular template on the dotted fabric and cut out a fabric circle. Using doubled polyester sewing thread, hand sew a line of running stitch ¼ in. (5mm) in from the edge of the fabric circle.

4 Gather the fabric into a yoyo by pulling the threads up tightly and securing them firmly with a few backstitches.

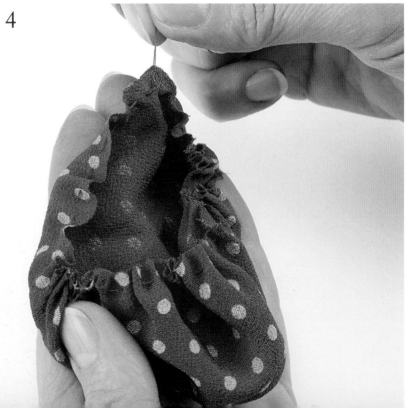

5

6

Assembling the flower

5 Place the leaves on the right side of the flower so that they protrude from the center out over the edge. Stitch them in place.

6 Stitch the dotted fabric yoyo over the leaves, positioning it in the center of the flower. Stitch through the fabric and felt layers to hold them all together.

7 Stitch two buttons stacked on top of one another into the center of the yoyo. Stitch several smaller buttons onto the surrounding fabric circle, placing one of them just over the edge onto the felt.

8 Finish by stitching a brooch back finding to the back of the flower, positioning it slightly towards the top so that the brooch sits well when you are wearing it.

7

8

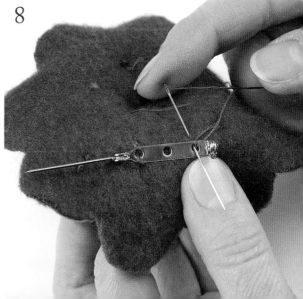

Templates

SCALE OF JEWELRY

Many of the pieces in this book are quite large in scale and may seem a little imposing for some wearers. Do adapt the projects to suit your own style in this respect. For many larger and taller people the scales will be correct, but if you are petite or dislike larger pieces of jewelry, then alter the measurements given to your choice.

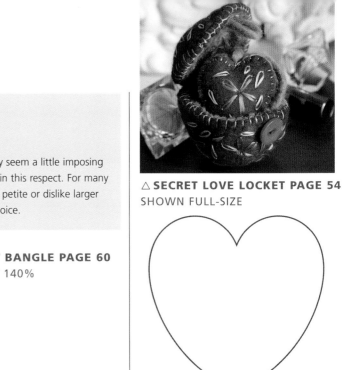

△ **SECRET LOVE LOCKET PAGE 54**
SHOWN FULL-SIZE

▽ **ABSTRACT BANGLE PAGE 60**
INCREASE BY 140%

△ **BUTTON FLOWER BROOCH PAGE 36**
INCREASE BY 200%

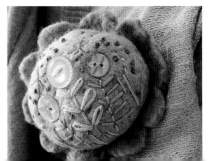

▽ **LEAF SHADOW SCARF PAGE 84**
INCREASE BY 290%

JOIN EDGES TOGETHER HERE

LARGE SPIKY DAHLIA = C1 + C2 + C3
SMALL SPIKY DAHLIA = A1 + C1 + C2
ROUND DAHLIA = B1 + B2

A

B

C

◁ **DAHLIA HEADDRESS PAGE 72**
INCREASE EACH AS INDICATED BELOW

A1 Increase by 220% x 1
B1 Increase by 240% x 1
B2 Increase by 275% x 1

C1 Increase by 280% x 2
C2 Increase by 300% x 1
C3 Increase by 350% x 2

▷ **FLUTED CORSAGE
AND HAIRGRIP PAGE 76**
INCREASE BY 200%

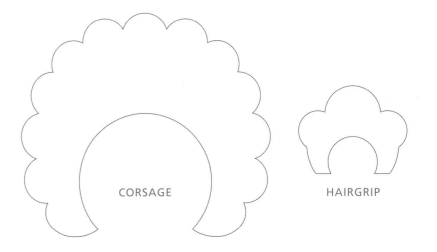

CORSAGE

HAIRGRIP

▷ **BIRD BROOCH PAGE 94**
INCREASE BY 150%

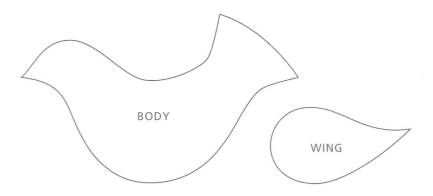

BODY

WING

▷ **FLOWER BROOCH PAGE 120**
INCREASE BY 200%

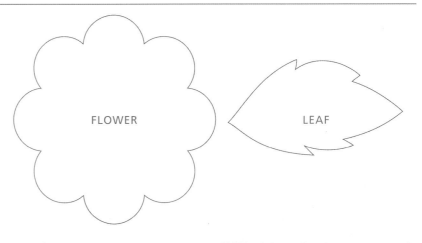

FLOWER

LEAF

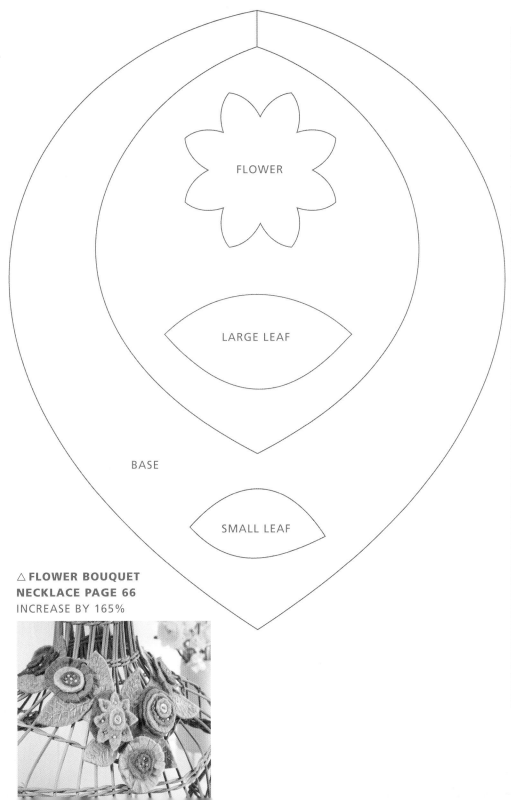

FLOWER

LARGE LEAF

BASE

SMALL LEAF

△ **FLOWER BOUQUET
NECKLACE PAGE 66**
INCREASE BY 165%

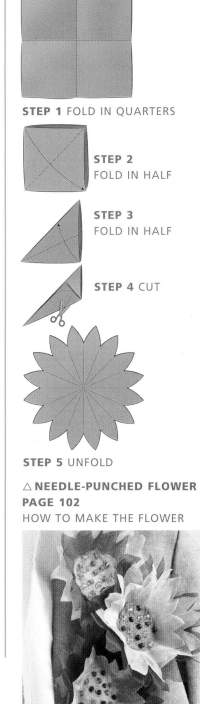

STEP 1 FOLD IN QUARTERS

STEP 2
FOLD IN HALF

STEP 3
FOLD IN HALF

STEP 4 CUT

STEP 5 UNFOLD

△ **NEEDLE-PUNCHED FLOWER
PAGE 102**
HOW TO MAKE THE FLOWER

Index

This index gives page references to the projects found in the book. Page numbers in italics refer to the main illustration. As many materials and techniques are used throughout the book, the page references are intended to direct the reader to substantial entries only.

A
Abstract Bangle 60-63, *61*
African Bangles 40-43, *41*
Anemone Ring 44-49, *45*

B
back stitch 37, *37*
barrettes see hair decorations
Beaded Felt Bracelet 20-25, *21*
Beaded Felt Necklace 25, *25*
beads 10, *10*
belt 80-83, *81*
Berry Brooch 25, *25*
Berry Necklace 25, *25*
Bird Brooch 94-97, *95*
blanket stitch 57, *57*
bracelets 20-25, 40-43, 60-63
braids 9, *9*
brooches 25, 36-39, 71, 75, 76-78, 94-97, 102-105, 120-123
Button Flower Brooch 36-39, *36*
buttons 10, *10*

C
Chunky Necklace 50-53, *51*
Cloud Scarf 106-109, *107*
corsages see brooches
cross-stitch 32, *32*

D
Dahlia Corsage 75, *75*
Dahlia Headdress 72-75, *73*
decorating felt 17-18, *17-18*
detached chain stitch 37, *37-38*
dissolvable film 15, *106*, *112*

E
earrings 33, *33*
embroidery
hand 18
free machine 17-18
equipment 11-12, *11-12*

F
fabrics 9, *9*
felt 8, *8*
felt beads 13, *13*
felted knitting 15
felting knitwear 16
findings 10, *10*
flat felt 13, *60-62*
Flower Bouquet Barrette 71, *71*
Flower Bouquet Brooch 71, *71*
Flower Bouquet Neckpiece 66-71, *67*
Flower Brooch 120-123, *121*
Fluted Corsage 76-78, *77*
Fluted Flower Hair Decorations 79, *79*
Folk Art Earrings 33, *33*
Folk Art Necklace 30-33, *31*
Folk Art Ring 33, *33*
free machine embroidery 17-18
french knots 32, *32-33*

H
hair decorations 71, 72-75, 79, 110-115
hand embroidery 18
health and safety 16, *18*
herringbone stitch 118, *118*

I
iPod or Phone Case 116-119, *117*

K
Knitted Neck Warmer 90-93, *91*
knotted stitches 17

L
Layered Circle Belt 80-83, *81*

lazy daisy stitch 57, *57-58*
Leaf Shadow Scarf 84-89, *85*

M
materials 8-10, *8-10*

N
necklaces 25, 26-29, 30-33, 34-35, 50-53, 54-59
neckwear 66-71, 84-89, 90-93, 98-101, 106-109
needle-punched felt 15, *104*
Needle-Punched Flower 102-105, *103*
nuno felt 14, *98-101*

P
patterning 14, *26*
Pebble Necklace 26-29, *27*
Phone or iPod case 116-119, *117*
processes 13-14

R
ribbons 9, *9*
rings 33, 44-49, 64-65
Rosy Nuno Scarf 98-101, *99*

S
scarves see neckwear
Sea-life Head Band 110-115, *111*
Secret Love Locket 54-59, *55*
stab stitch 38, *38*
star stitch 32, *32*
straight stitch 106

T
techniques 13-16, *13-16*
templates 124-127
threads 9, *9*
Tie-dye Necklace 34-35, *35*
Tower Ring 64-65, *65*

Z
zigzag stitch 106

Acknowledgments

Thanks and appreciation to: Steve, my partner, again your love, patience, philosophy, and humor have seen me through another book and a challenging year.

Gracie Cooper and Sue Lucas for passing on their valuable felt-making knowledge to me at various times.

My students at various colleges in Bristol and Bath, England, for your endless enthusiasm, inspiration, and love of all things felted.

Mum and Dad for passing on your skills and love of making things. I'm very grateful that I have spent almost every day of my working life being creative in some way.

All my friends and family for your much-valued support and feedback, as well as understanding the infrequency of my social appearances.

Lizzie Orme for the gorgeous photographs and friendly encouragement. Elizabeth Healey for her fantastic design skills. Janet Ravenscroft, Paula Breslich, and Jane Birch at Breslich & Foss for your patience, support, and enthusiasm for my ideas and for making them happen!